UNUSUAL CIRCUMSTANCES, INTERESTING TIMES

UNUSUAL CIRCUMSTANCES, INTERESTING TIMES

And Other Impolite Interventions

BRIAN FAWCETT

New Star Books   1991

Thanks go to Stan Persky for talking me into collecting these essays (and for forcing me to discover what a one-track mind I have), and to Rolf Maurer for showing up with the catalogue copy just as I was about to decide I really ought to take one last shot at becoming a professional baseball player. Thanks also to Steve Wells and Carmen Mills for editorial help. Office space was provided by the Four Wings Café, the Vineyard Restaurant, and Café Crème in Vancouver, and various Golden Griddle outlets around Yonge and Eglinton in Toronto.

I would somewhat humbly like to dedicate all this to the memory of George Orwell. Many of the remarkable things he said and did have influenced this book. I can claim, at the very least, that I have met his indirect challenge to write a book without using semicolons.   – BF

Printed on PH-neutral paper
Printed and bound in Canada
First printing November 1991
1 2 3 4 5   95 94 93 92 91

Editing and production: Rolf Maurer, Jean Kavanagh, Audrey McClellan
Cover design and illustration: David Lester

Publication of this book is made possible by grants from the Canada Council and the Cultural Services Branch, Province of British Columbia

Cataloguing in Publication Data

Fawcett, Brian, 1944-
Unusual circumstances, interesting times

Essays which originally appeared in various publications.
Includes index.
ISBN 0-921586-27-2

I. Title.
PS8561.A94U5 1991   C814'.54   C91-091680-2
PR9199.3.F39U5 1991

New Star Books Ltd.
2504 York Avenue
Vancouver, B.C.
V6K 1E3

CONTENTS

Part 2: FOR CIVIL INTERVENTIONS

UNUSUAL CIRCUMSTANCES, INTERESTING TIMES

INTRODUCTION

This book tracks a relatively limited number of ideas about the way Canadians live and work as political and creative beings. Throughout, I'm suggesting that while we're enthusiastically committed to the privileges of western traditions, most of us are failing to accept the public and private responsibilities inherent in the intellectual and political methods that secure that tradition. In a sense, what is at stake isn't a tradition at all, but a dynamic process that requires systematic re-evaluation and renovation. The past tells us that to the extent that this process remains dynamic, the result is political democracy (warts and all) and individual creativity. Where it doesn't, it seems to me, the result is arbitrary authority, ideological fundamentalisms, and social violence.

Over the last fifteen years I've become convinced that professionalism and technocratic expertise (particularly in the field of communications) have become reactionary forces that are moving against both democratic practice and artistic creativity. Most of the book consists of successive and progressive attempts to define and contextualize the effects of those phenomena.

Part One is mainly concerned with writing, and with the responsibilities of writers and other artists. Lodged within it is a serial jeremiad about how, through incompetence and lazy acceptance of professional privilege, our literary forms are ceasing to be much more than a glittery, irrelevant forest of ossified aesthetic artifacts meant to dress up the lives of a few middle-class antiquarians and fetishists. Part Two of the book is very much concerned with the failure of professionalism and expertise, but it focuses more on the civil and political manifestations of the same troubling set of phenomena, particularly in architecture.

All but one of the essays here were first published in anthologies, journals, magazines or newspapers in Canada and the U.S. Most of them bear only a rudimentary resemblance to the originals, partly because I'm an inveterate and compulsive revisionist, and partly because the demands of a book are quite different from those made by an isolated piece of writing. Although two of the essays were first written for *NMFG* in the mid-1970s, most of them were written after 1985, when the indirectness of fiction and other conventional genre behaviours began to seem far too slow for the cultural and political crises confronting us. As a concession to archivists, I've indicated at the end of each essay where it was originally published, but have not noted the year because the revisions are generally so extensive that setting them at their original point of composition or publication would be misleading. If I thought that archivists were going to be as important in the future as they have been in the recent past, I'd have been more careful. But I haven't ever kept records of what I write, and the way things are going, doing so seems even less worth the effort today. Readers should therefore date all the essays at 1991, and judge them accordingly.

This is not always a polite book, and for that I make no apology. A long time ago I discovered that all writers must make a choice between trying to become wealthy and popular and trying to tell the truth. I chose the latter and the choice, once made, seems to be binding. And anyway, if I'd wanted to drive a BMW and spend my intelligence bending over to kiss patches of redolent but influential skin, I would have gone into real estate or weapons development. I didn't and I don't. Consequently, the often-greasy "other hand" is occasionally absent from these essays.

Vancouver
October, 1991

Part I:
AGAINST
PRIVATE
INVENTIONS

STARTING
OVER AGAIN

The day after my last volume of verse was published in 1982 I had an experience that made me start over again as a writer. The book in question, *Aggressive Transport*, was seven years in composition. As volumes of contemporary verse go, it was quite large (132 pages), and it was ambitious enough to try to carry a narrative that interlocked the individual poems throughout the entire text. I was proud of what I'd done, and the moment my publisher phoned to say that they had copies from the printer, I rushed down to pick up a box so I could deliver the books – on consignment – to the few bookstores in Vancouver I knew would take them. But just as I was about to enter the first bookstore, I stopped. I couldn't think of a single person who would really want to read my book.

There were a few who I knew would buy it, but that wasn't quite the same thing. They'd buy it out of a sense of obligation, either to support my work specifically or to support what they regard as "local literary activity". Neither of those motives struck me as very good ones. When I gave it a little thought, I discovered that I didn't believe that more than maybe half of those dozen or so obligatory buyers would actually read the book. Most important, I discovered that I really couldn't blame them, or any of the 25 million or so others in Canada who wouldn't buy my book at all. What I was bringing to the bookstore simply wasn't readable.

Let me clarify. *Aggressive Transport* could (and still can) be read, enjoyed and understood – given some specialized skills. Furthermore, the book was (and still is) *worthy* of being read. It is skilfully written, occasionally moving, and perhaps even brilliant in several passages. Writing the poems and composing the book was an act of cultural courage on my part – just as is the case with most of the other volumes of verse that sit, unread, on the shelves of those bookstores that still carry them. Letting *Aggressive Transport* be *published*, was, however, an act of cultural bravado on my part.

Bravado is not the same thing as courage. Deeds of courage are committed by people who act consciously on principle or respond actively to a situation with the knowledge that the risks they take – of limb, psychic safety or life – do not serve their immediate self-interest. Courageous people know that life under the bed is safe but slimey. But bravado is grounded in ignorance or stupidity – the act of a person who, say, jumps into a bullring believing that what he will meet there will be a chicken or that bulls are gentle, sensible creatures that will respond positively to kindness and reason.

I didn't go into the bookstore. Instead, I walked around the block and let the revelation sink in. Sure, every poet I knew did the same thing I'd been about to do. So what? I couldn't avoid the sensation that walking into that bookstore would be another act of bravado, and that I should think it over.

Again, don't get me wrong. I am not implying that writing poetry is a worthless activity. It is a valuable activity in a number of ways. It is, for instance, a much better thing to be doing than selling drugs or real estate or dumping toxic wastes into our dying waterways. Poetry is a fundamental human activity, and has been since the origins of language. At some point in their life, almost everyone attempts to write poetry, now – unfortunately – usually only at points of private emotional crisis. Frankly, I'd take it a step further. Notwithstanding the use individuals currently make of it, poetry is perhaps the most profound manifestation of human imagination that exists, and it is one of the most powerful tools human intelligence has ever devised – the act from which nearly all civilized behaviours have derived. It is a great shame that most people have ceased to read poetry, and a much greater shame that its methods are no longer practised in a disciplined way by citizens as part of their daily lives.

I'm not exaggerating in the least when I say that some of the deepest pleasures life has provided for me have come while I have been writing or reading poetry, and that I cannot imagine living a life that does not have poetry somewhere near its centre. That being declared, I can't any longer see any reason for continuing to publish verse. Today fewer people read poetry than write it, and still fewer people see the publication of verse as anything more than an obligatory response to composition or to the availability of government programs to fund its publication.

There are a number of reasons why poetry has become unreadable. Some are the fault of the poets, and others are attributable to the peculiar conditions of contemporary culture and the more peculiar interrelations between contemporary culture, economics and technology that have emerged in the 20th century. Looking at those reasons isn't going to be pleasant. I'm going to try anyway, and after I've done so, I'd like to make some modest proposals about how those who write poetry might want to respond to this fix.

My decision not to enter the bookstore wasn't the result of any sudden, mystical revelation. During the year or so while I was finishing *Aggressive Transport*, I was also teaching creative writing for the University of Victoria in B.C.'s federal penitentiaries. The idea behind the program I taught in, which offered a variety of liberal arts courses, was that most criminals aren't crazy or evil, but rather that they're culturally miseducated, or, more accurately, that they haven't been educated at all. As prisoners of society, they have had the same rights and duties of democratic citizenship officially withdrawn that were denied them by their ignorance in the first place.

Most of the verse I saw in my classes was awful. But it was awful in a very specific way, and it was that specificity that quickly determined my teaching methods, and eventually began to alter my outlook.

Prisons – anywhere and in any epoch – are paradigms of the society that builds and uses them. The value systems prison inmates hold, provided that they aren't psychopathic, are exact if exaggerated models of the cultural psychologies and core values of the larger society that has isolated the inmates from the general public. Consequently, it didn't take me long to figure out that my students were labouring under pretty much the same set of assumptions about writing as most people who enroll in university creative writing classes. The chief assumptions were that self-expression is automatically worthwhile, and that language is a tool to be manipulated toward that end, particularly if it is economically lucrative to do so.

My inmate-students' chief reason for writing was to express what they *felt* about the people, objects, and ideas around them. The range of their feeling was startlingly normal even if the arrangements and assigned characteristics of objects, people, and ideas were sometimes pretty weird. My students expressed alienation, aggression, desire, sadness, omniscience, happiness – in about that order of intensity and frequency. But it was what they *did not think about* in their expressive forays that quickly began to interest me most.

Generally speaking, my students felt utterly no responsibility toward the subject matter or the audience for their writings, and they had little interest in recognizing possible historical and political relationships between their use of materials, themselves and others. Respect for the integrity of external materials wasn't part of their concept of social and artistic responsibility. Actually, most of them had no coherent concept of social or artistic responsibility at all because the relationships between their own identities and those of others – including the identity of ideas – had no boundaries. Where any relationships existed they were imprinted much the same way as they are, say, in an iguana responding to its own image in a mirror – paranoiacally. Respecting external identities and properties simply wasn't included in their formula of self-expression.

That's worth looking at carefully, because it isn't a flaw in the personalities of the individual inmates, and it's not a failure of the prison system or of the criminal justice system. It's much more important and profound. It's a signal of collapse within the fabric of our whole damned civilization – its value structure, its educational system and its techniques for socializing citizens. This may be the first civilization in history to produce its own barbarians, and certainly the first to install them into positions of influence and power throughout the political and social structure.

Despite having committed crimes, my students were not abnormal specimens of humanity. On the contrary, they were almost supernormal – instances of social normality unmediated by individual intervention. Self-irony, reflective evaluation of experience, and the other apparatuses of civilized self-control were simply not functioning in these people. Many of them were in jail because they'd bought into the value system of contemporary society as if it were a consumer romp in a supermarket. And a consumer romp is pretty well the way we're all encouraged to see this society. They'd chosen whatever values and behaviours suited their appetites and their immediate interests and rejected the rest of the package. They didn't recognize that they had social duties and personal restraints, and therefore had reacted to situations with a combination of inaccurate self-interest, blind ignorance and, frequently, violence. That's what it is to be culturally underprivileged or handicapped.

I tried, as a teacher, to suggest to them that poetry was first and finally an engagement with civilization and with a tradition that goes back well beyond modern civilization. I gave them Gilgamesh, Homer, Hesiod, Dante and anything else I could scrounge up that

might force them out of the notion that they were all alone in a supermarket, and that poetry was merely a vehicle for the unbridled
expression of their isolated emotions, opinions and perceptions.

In most cases I got nowhere. All I had with them was five hours a
week and the evidence of a lot of dead poets – most of whom were
thoroughly unsuccessful individuals in modern terms – and one or
two equally unsuccessful live ones I brought in to talk to them. None
of the poets I introduced to them had money, Corvettes, expensive
clothing or massive amounts of drugs to sell or ingest. I was up
against the prison the inmates lived with the other 163 hours a week,
and an experience of civilization that had told them – by telling them
nothing at all – pretty much the opposite of what the poets said.

Only one geniune poet emerged out of those classes, along with
perhaps a dozen more who were affected in other ways by what they
learned there. But we had some classroom arguments that were usually interesting and occasionally pretty athletic. It was during these
arguments that I learned a number of things about my chosen voca-
tion and its craft that I now can't ignore.

I've come to believe that poetry is first and finally a tool of historical, intellectual and emotional investigation, and that the "tradition"
of poetry is merely the record of that investigation – not a museum of
pristine aesthetic artifacts or a collection of eternal wisdoms. Poets
likewise are themselves never more – nor less – than the agents of
that ongoing investigation. If that seems excessively abstract, have
another look. I think it was the American poet Leroi Jones (now
Amiri Baraka) who pointed out that art is about thought, not the other
way round. Poetry started because human beings needed more successful ways to perceive and think about the world – ways that would
engage deeper complexities and prevent the violence that is the inevitable result of not being able to think successfully or relevantly.
Whatever form it appears in, poetry is a psychotechnical device
designed to enhance perception. It's an intellectual method, and we
need such things more today than ever before.

On a personal note, about the same time as I was clarifying my
ideas about the role of poetry I started to realize that the parameters of

my own poetic investigations were uncomfortably similar to those of my students. I'd rarely ventured beyond the boundaries of obscure self-expression, and the language I was using reflected that. The investigations of my fellow professional poets began to seem equally narrow.

Let me emphasize what we're all supposed to know: that ideas, emotions, and events exist in context, and in a social fabric. Any poet who abandons the responsibility of understanding and interpreting the contextual fabric of their materials is in effect abandoning both those materials and poetry itself. Granted, the complexity of modern civilization makes it an essentially absurd task. It has probably been that way since the 16th century. So what?

Let me also emphasize that this is not a partisan call for topicality or propaganda. It is a demand for the opposite: for what Rilke called "invisibility" and what Mayakovsky called "the social command". It is one of the first demands that the old muses make of a poet. Those who do not respond to it accurately will find their work lodged in irrelevance.

So what, specifically, is wrong with contemporary poetry? Well, how about an analogy. Imagine a group of structural engineers discussing their work. One of them criticizes the riveting strength of beams in a foundation that is going to hold a 30-storey building stable. The pattern, says the first engineer, is idiosyncratic; there are not enough rivets, or the rivets are too small. Worse, connecting crossbeams are needed in several places to keep the building from collapsing. Several other engineers offer similar interventions. The engineer in charge of the building under examination calmly answers their criticisms by saying that the design is his own, and that he's done things the way he has because he likes the look and feel of it. The key elements are inspirational in origin – they came to him in the night, and to him, the design *feels* right.

That's the way most poets talk about their work. You may want to argue that the parallel I'm making doesn't apply, because poetry isn't *about* anything material. It is only language, and that is a private matter, between the poet and his or her muse. Poets work alone, and they operate with intangible materials of the self. Objective interventions don't matter, right? Wrong.

The contemporary unwillingness of poets to discuss the sources and technology of composition – or the willingness to cloud it with silly mystical notions of inspiration – is a mind-boggling irony considering that those same poets are cheerfully willing to declare themselves expert practitioners of language.

I don't want to sound simple-minded, but a very large part of the problem is that too many poets don't work hard enough. This is a complicated argument to try to make, because it appears to attack the spiritual integrity of a lot of nice people, and because the exceptions are many. But I'm making a pragmatic observation here, not lodging a spiritual attack. In this culture, most poets are forced to write in their spare time. Like most people, they have to work at proletarianized jobs in order to live. In Canada, a startling number of poets are employed as university and college teachers. They don't write as much as they'd like to (and should) because they have papers to mark, classes to prepare. They need a new Volvo, the children need dental braces or ballet lessons.

Somewhere in the nexus of those kinds of bourgeois priorities, a decision gets made about the importance of poetry, such that the poetry that gets written is "academic" – which is to say, it is carried on in ways that do not put those cherished day-to-day priorities at risk. Academia is not, as is generally supposed, a sanctuary for disinterested metaphysical contemplation of life and nature. Greek history tells us that the Groves of Academe was the estate of an Athenian traitor named Academus. The estate was spared by the invading Spartan armies because Academus and some of his friends operated as a fifth column for them. They betrayed their city so that they could retain their privileged status, and Athens was brutally plundered as a result.

Academic poetry is a disease caused by the refusal or inability to investigate and take responsibility for the complexity of the context in which poetic composition takes place. It is not enough for poets to partition off and then exploit a small corner of reality. Poets must be prepared to investigate all aspects of the reality they inhabit. The production of poems as aesthetically competent and formally closed artifacts should be secondary to the research involved in poetry, and to the discourse that a poem should propose – its intellectual method, so to speak. It isn't.

The current irrelevance of poetry isn't entirely the fault of the poets. The Global Village, which Marshall McLuhan predicted in the late 1950s, is now upon us, and it is not a nutritive context for poetry. The natural attentions of poetry, in fact, are inimical to the methods of experiencing the world and the self that are popular and expedient in the Global Village.

The Global Village has altered the nature and purpose of information, and it orders perception into commercially manipulatable modes. It increases the volume of information and binarizes it, but radically reduces its density. Simultaneously it has massively increased the number and variety of reception and transmission points. We are encouraged, tacitly, to accumulate, consume and experience information, and at the same time discouraged from analyzing it with any degree of cohesion or depth. For the unsophisticated, the apparent availability of information may seem an advantage – until one begins to understand that the advantages go to the technologically privileged, and that even then, the ability to accumulate masses of low-density information leaves untouched the question of how to accurately or usefully interpret it.

Together with some of my writing students in the prison, I worked out a definition of poetry that illuminates its functional demands, accounts for its tradition, and points to the ways in which it involves perceptual procedures that are radically contrary to those of the Global Village: *Poetry is the shortest conduit between two linguistic points that accounts for the non-linguistic complexity of the passage.*

In fact, the perceptual techniques of such a poetry would be uniquely valuable in combatting the disintegrations of intelligence and memory that seem to be the goal of Global Village social and perceptual technologies. Traditionally, poetry has been the voice of the particular and of the sacred – "sacred" defined in the strict anthropological sense as those elements of existence having to do with communal and public life.

The Global Village is a massive, indirect but deliberate attack on the particular and on the sacred. It is breaking down Euro-American civilization into a series of binary consumer enclaves: groups of citizens who build their cultural lives around the consumption and manipulation of ideas, products and activities. These enclaves seem to be of two distinct kinds: affective and reflective.

An "affective" enclave – such as that of the media or, say, the legal profession – is characterized by a style and social rhetoric that satisfies the needs of its members for social dignity and identity, while at the same time influencing other enclaves. It does this either by controlling the flow of ideas and information, by arbitrating values (directly or indirectly) or by setting standards for social behaviour.

Most enclaves are simply reflective or imitative. Food, personal health and even sports enthusiasts can enjoy a more or less self-contained and self-sustaining lifestyle centred around their chosen activity. Curiously enough, many enclaves based on religious or business and even political ideas – enclaves that one would assume would operate affectively – operate reflectively. In the Global Village it doesn't matter whether you're interested in tennis or Armageddon; you are there to consume (and be consumed by) the infinite and isolating variety of manufactured commodities.

Poetry is becoming, or has already become, a reflective enclave. Certainly this has already happened to other enclaves within the arts, particularly those which have been mainly concerned with defending their formal boundaries against what they perceive – accurately or not – as the vulgarity of contemporary life. Classical music, opera and ballet are obvious instances.

It is true that poets have remained the defenders of particularity, but to do that without an active engagement with matters of public language and form makes them at best no more than antiquarians and Kabbalarians. At worst, they become a convenient release mechanism for "unproductive" elements of the human psyche – a utility of the Global Village, and probably a temporary one.

What is occurring across North America and Europe is the atomization of human social intelligence, a breaking down of social forms into increasingly alienated and easy-to-manipulate cells. A large part of that breakdown, obviously, is going on within language. And while I am not suggesting that poets should man the barricades or write poems denouncing the bad news, I am suggesting that poets are not doing much – formally or otherwise – to address the crisis. It is urgent that poets begin doing just that. In a few years, the Global Village, for reasons of economic scarcity, may cease to be as liberal as it is today. It might do away with the subsidy structures that support the publication of poetry, consign the literature departments of the universities to the museums, and it will all be over.

I'd rather start over on my own.

1. To begin with, I would like to make a distinction between poetry, which *is* essential to human well-being, and verse, which is merely the technical form in which much of poetry has seen expression for a few thousand years.

I'm not sure that verse as we know it would disappear if poets practised their art as a radical essential of human thought and were less reactionary – and more circumspect – about defending poetic forms against all comers and changing technology. Probably it wouldn't disappear altogether, at least not for a while. But I have a sneaking suspicion that if poets were keeping pace with technological change, a good chunk of the poetry of our time would look more like television commercials and rock videos than the tiny, perfect one-page poems that fill our (largely unread) literary journals. No poet is required to fall in love with technology, but ignoring it completely isn't a competent defence of the muses. I try to imagine Homer refusing to write down the Odyssey and Iliad on the grounds that he (or she) preferred to stick with oral technology. I try to, but I can't.

2. Can we please get rid of the self-serving notion that writers of verse are public poets in the manner of Homer, Pindar or the troubadours of the Middle Ages? It just ain't so. The general public just doesn't love us the same way. I'm not sure whether it's because of the degeneration of the public realm in the past centuries, or because of the growth of mass stateism, or because poetry operates at a level of particularity that has become (alas!) temporarily incomprehensible to most people. But I'm really tired of jerks who make fools of themselves in public by crashing political rallies to read their diaries or chant their mantras, and then berate other poets for not doing the same and whine constantly about how the government doesn't love them when the public does. The government isn't supposed to love poets, and the public consists of quite a lot of people – more than the twenty who go to free poetry readings on Sunday afternoons, or the ten or fifteen who might really understand poetry when it is read or chanted or sung at a political rally.

If there are public poets in the latter part of the 20th century, then they are those few popular song-writer/performers who also happen to write lyrics that make sense – a rare combination in the music world. Currently, Canada has several of these kinds of poets. Joni Mitchell, Bruce Cockburn and Leonard Cohen come quickly to mind.

3. Since I'm not much of a guitarist and I don't like crowds, I'm going to (therefore) focus on poetry as an intellectual method located (at least for now) primarily in written (or printed) language, and give up the illusion that it is either a popular public activity or a valued kind of disembodied aesthetic product.

There's nothing wrong, of course, with an artist either wanting or actively seeking public recognition. My hope is that the unreadability of poetry is temporary. But right now, a poet who seeks wide public recognition for his or her verse is either chronically whacked on drugs, stupid, operating under mysterious control mechanisms from outer space, or is prepared to write greeting card materials. He or she is also misapplying their attentions and skills.

There are good reasons to continue to operate from written and printed language, and there are equally good reasons for poets to continue to think and write. Electronic technology has yet to provide a format that allows leisurely, idiosyncratic individual interaction with information. Text alone affords that. Such interactions are what produce competent intellectual methods – the kinds that can provide us with passage from both linguistic, perceptual and discursive points with a full accounting of the complexities encountered. That is the gift poetry offers to individuals, and it is the service it provides to human civilization. Poetry is valuable, regardless of whether individuals or societies can at any given moment acknowledge it, because poetry is (still) an essential mode of thought.

Implicit in everything I've said about the importance of poetry is the idea that it is first and foremost an intellectual method, and only secondarily a communications medium. I'm asking that we begin to focus on poetry as a means of interpreting and tuning reality, and that we let the comforts and privileges of current forms of expression begin their long-overdue transformation.

4. Can we publish less? Books are wonderful things. But there are far too many books of poetry being published. I know of no one able to keep up with the annual output of them, not even in the universities, where keeping track of them should be – but isn't – part of the English department's scholarly responsibility.

If someone can produce a competent (i.e. non-opportunistic) argument for continuing to publish the quantities of verse currently being published under the illusion that poetry is a relevant market commodity, I would like to hear it. Meanwhile, most of the books that are published are being published for lousy reasons. Often it is because a poet has amassed a significant number of magazine publications in college literary journals. Sometimes it is because an academic C.V. needs to have new additions made to it, or a growing one needs to be filled out. Sometimes it is because a new poet needs a publication in order to break into the various subsidy programs. Lousy reasons, all.

Some of the literary presses are to blame for the over-abundance of books. A few of them don't even bother to edit the individual poems, and everyone has seen volumes of poems that haven't even been proof-read. More destructively, most of the presses make no attempt to establish a coherent narrative within the body of the text, so that the books *can't* be read as books. From there, the publishers publicize their products half-heartedly, and distribute them with equal indifference, as if their responsibilities ended when the book arrives at the warehouse. One can't help suspecting that part of the motive for publishing so much verse is simple laziness. Typesetting and layout for poetry is cheaper and easier than for prose. There are fewer words in a book of poetry, and only the left margin needs to be justified.

If the situation is going to improve, the poets ought to take the first steps. They should begin by accepting a greater degree of responsibility for what they're putting in front of the reading public. Most poets know how to write a lyric poem, but that isn't enough. They should compose their manuscripts more rigorously. Next, the publishers should edit manuscripts with the same degree of rigour. And they should publicize and distribute the books they do publish with a lot more energy and commitment than they are doing. Is this too much to ask? If it is too much, then we should all be prepared to ask ourselves why.

5. Here is a very specific proposal (I intend to include my own poetry in this). *Every published poet in Canada should take a ten-year moratorium on the publication of his or her next book of poems.* Poets are in a unique situation, one in which they could turn the visible disadvantages into a profound advantage. No one – meaning the general public – seems able to read poetry right now. Poetry sales have been declining across the English-speaking world for more than a decade, and the average sales of individual volumes is less than 300 copies. Since no one is reading, why not turn this privacy

from public scrutiny to a real privacy, and use it to compose better poems and better books of poetry?

I'm not suggesting that poets stop writing. I haven't stopped, and I don't intend to. I'm just suggesting that instead of publishing into a vacuum, poets should withhold their work, let it cook longer. Over ten years, a poet who works hard should be able to distill his or her poems into deeper levels of coherence and understanding, and will inevitably practise a selectivity that, with the opportunities that now exist for premature publication, probably isn't possible. Sure, ten years is a long time. But Paul Valéry once took twenty years off both writing and publishing just to *think* about poetry. If ten years seems too long to wait, perhaps eager-to-publish poets might try measuring the quality of their work against his, and publish accordingly. New poets should be allowed a first publication, of course. But with the prospect of a ten-year wait before the next publication, the result will almost certainly be better first books.

The publication of chapbooks and magazines should be encouraged, but only on an unsubsidized basis. This would force publication levels and print values downward, and hopefully into some measure that relates to actual demand. One result would almost certainly be the disappearance of some marginal literary publishers, and the disappearance of several glossy low-volume periodicals. That will save a few innocent trees, and more important, it will return chapbook and periodical activity to its natural purpose – enabling the intellectual and technical development of poetic skills and furthering discourse among working poets.

The Bumper Book

WHAT IS LITERATURE FOR?

Occasionally a book will raise questions it has neither the intention of asking nor the capacity to answer. Usually this happens when the author is naive or has taken a stand on some issue he or she doesn't quite have the goods on. Sometimes it happens simply because the author is a technically incompetent writer. When it is the latter, the questions raised are rarely very interesting. But when the book involved has serious pretensions and when the questions arise from the author's naive ambition, the issues involved are invariably political and philosophical. Usually they concern the nature and practice of good and evil, which are supposedly at the heart of literature's subject matter.

A recent book of stories I happened across, written by Canadian university literature instructor Eric McCormack and titled *Inspecting the Vaults*, raises a whole lot of unintentional questions about the theory and practice of good and evil. They're questions the author and his text seem neither interested in nor able to answer. What I have to say about this book, therefore, is going to seem totally unfair to the no doubt genteel and witty and very nice Eric McCormack. But the questions *Inspecting the Vaults* raises are very serious ones.

I came to this book in utter good faith. Several writers I respect told me it was very good, and I even went out and *purchased* it at a bookstore (I'm a patriotic kind of guy, a simple barbarian from northern British Columbia, and so I buy books instead of waiting around for free desk or review copies). Eric McCormack is a new writer, or at least newly discovered by Penguin Books, the press responsible for discovering Plato, the Greek dramatists, and William Shakespeare. McCormack should be supported, I thought. And maybe he can show me some ideas and tricks I haven't seen before.

Unfortunately I was wrong on both those counts. McCormack shouldn't be supported, and even though he writes with a degree of technical skill, the only thing that appears to be inventive about this book is that it manages to be naive and perverse at the same time. And that's only an appearance. But I'm jumping ahead of myself.

I read the title story first, and with all my receptors wide open, hoping to like what I read. Sure enough, it fulfilled several of the promises in the jacket copy. It was imaginative, improbably sexy, and it was disturbingly macabre. Right on target on those items. McCormack's prose was, as one of the jacket blurbs promised, at least dramatically controlled if not entirely flawless. And I was, to be honest, unsettled, both by the story and by the writer's talent – again, just as the dust-jacket copy promised I would be.

Unfortunately, I wasn't unsettled for quite the reasons the jacket copy suggested I should be. Running afoul of the English department by being unable to suspend disbelief, I was wondering, in a kind of dumbfounded way, why McCormack had written the story.

When, for instance, Franz Kafka wrote *The Castle*, he was attempting to delineate, in a state of considerable agony and desperation, the nature and methods of bureaucratic terror. But in McCormack's tale, which seems to have debts to Kafka's now-generic explication of the subject, I can feel distinct traces of the Kafka mood and diction, but there is no detectable desperation anywhere in the tale. McCormack was enjoying himself. Equally disturbing, the metaphors employed seem more tied to literary texts for authentication rather than (as in Kafka) to perceived world realities. As a matter of record, the main referent in the story appears to be the writings of Franz Kafka himself – with a little Jorge Luis Borges and Gabriel Garcia Marquez tossed in to, by turn, lighten and eroticize the impact.

I moved on from tale to tale, and with each one I became a little more disturbed. Eventually (just short of psychosis), a truer response developed – annoyance. By the time I was half way through the book, I was thoroughly angry and frustrated. In each tale, essential elements were missing. It was always the same ones, but just precisely which they were eluded me for a while.

Sure, the stories are reasonably well written, and they're entertaining, in a slippery, perverted sort of way. But they're empty stories. Where there should be a deeper range of meaning or even a sense of mystery, there is a gleeful exploitation of the penetralia of human ugliness and our collective tendency toward wacky and cruel behaviour.

After a few days of bedtime reading, I was ready to write the book off as a hybrid between *Nightmare on Elm Street* and *The Twilight Zone* – a not very profound or amusing collection of anecdotes about human obtuseness. But Eric McCormack's clicky prose wouldn't let me write it off. It kept dialing up the same international numbers and then hanging up the minute anything answered. Mainly, it was Kafka, Borges, and Garcia Marquez on the line. I became convinced that I was reading the work of an academic technician with considerable erudition and skill as a prose writer, but with the intellectual interests of one of the sicko tabloids' freak section editors.

Too easy, I decided. Something about this book was serious, and it was seriously wrong. So I veered off to examine McCormack's dial-a-famous-author reference bank. First, I asked myself what the difference is between Franz Kafka and Jorge Luis Borges, leaving aside the thornier question of Garcia Marquez for subsequent investigation. Unlike Kafka, whose intellectual enquiry was an ultimate one that sought out and described some of the structural fundamentals of mass civilization, Borges was the quintessential academic dilettante, a purveyor of carefully de-ideologized intellectual party favours and tricks.

I'm committing heresy by saying these things, I know. Okay, so fuck you too. I am simply *not* taken in by this schmarmy little library wart. I'm even glad he's finally dead and gone, although I know that for the next decade we'll be deluged by critical studies, biographies and posthumous writing from the academic industry built up around his reputation. I'm glad he's gone because at least there will be no more of those self-serving interviews with him in which he makes ludicrously humble-pie pronouncements about how books are world enough for any author, and how his ancestors did all kinds of terrible things to the poor – and how, since he isn't a man of action, he can ignore them, or, if it serves his purpose, paint up these gold chain-wearing macho bozos in colourful costumes and charm us with them.

In addition, now that Borges is dead we won't have to hear how his blindness frees his imagination from the unpleasantness of the present, or hear him say that Robert Louis Stevenson was as great a practitioner of the English language as William Shakespeare. Borges was an ignorant and dangerous man who has done incalculable damage to literature, and I'm glad the horrible bug-eyed mole is dead.

Now that I have my foot firmly planted adjacent to my speech organs, let me trace some of the effects of the virus that Borges, all unwittingly of course, let loose in Western literature. To begin, I want to take a slight step back from what I just said and see if I can take an accurate measure of what Borges did achieve as a writer – as opposed to railing about what his fans have made out of him.

Jorge Luis Borges was a technically skilled, if extremely minor writer whose only legitimate claim to glory is that he concocted several delicious intellectual puzzles. His story about Pierre Menard, a man who undertook to write a masterpiece as great as Cervantes' *Don Quixote* and succeeded only by duplicating it word for word, is a marvellous illustration of a minor aesthetic principle: that singular works of art are products of the historical parameters and contexts the author is lodged in, not the sidestream chromium from a timeless and magical elixir called inspiration. Similarly, Borges' anecdote about the Babylonian lottery is an almost-profound paradigm of what happens when a society becomes so engrossed in what it is doing that it forgets why it does it.

Most of Borges' other, less successful anecdotes and stories are like that: they promise mysterious significances but rarely deliver meaning that goes deeper than old wives' tales do. He's like Kahlil Gibran with Spanish castanets and crossword puzzles. Seen in the proper perspective, his writings have really served as nursery rhymes for a generation of permanently adolescent academics who have come to believe that art and the human mind are essentially obscure and that this obscurity is a commodity that can be elaborated and mystified with intellectual impunity – and as a dandy career vehicle. Borges' work – fluffy in substance and not too voluminous – is the perfect raw material for these frauds, who really just want to operate their industry without fear of the government or their colleagues catching on that they don't know piss from cowboy boots and don't care to.

To be generous to poor old Borges, it is this fan club that is the true problem. During the 1960s and 70s, Borges became the hero of a now-aging but culturally and academically dominant generation of young academic writers and teachers. These people were nice enough, but they were pure products of a system that was expanding too rapidly to maintain its standards. They were (and remain) what I've come to call DFIs: Default Intellectuals.

DFIs are people who in other generations would have been low-level bureaucrats and entrepreneurs. They don't value thought for its own sake, and in general, they are more interested in having private professional careers and secure salaries than in scholarship or in improving public education. Fearful of their own yawning mediocrity, armed with a self-serving relativism in which the value of any intellectual pursuit is relative to the curriculum vitae points it provides, and with Borges as a convenient role model, the DFIs in our university literature departments have set out to muddy the natural boundaries between philoprogenitive virtuosity and socially and intellectually responsive art, between criticism and literature, and between fact, fiction and received truth. They've successfully separated literature from the investigations going on in other scholarly disciplines, and they've undermined the credibility of literature as a cultural force.

On the whole, this generation of academic careerists are technologists rather than investigators – which is to say, they are prone to apply their technology without any attempt to uncover and identify verities that refer outside the narrow assumptions which dictate their technology. They're finally just as divorced from reality as those microbiologists who have made secure careers creating and nurturing lethal bacteria and viruses that if released would wipe out intelligent life on this planet within a week.

The academic careerists revere language, but like their microbiologist counterparts do with applied science, they use language merely as a multifaceted tool capable of creating phenomenal realities that are independent from sensible material and mass reality, about which they make it a virtue of knowing as little as possible beyond investment portfolios and pension plans. They are uninterested in the structures through which capitalism and its governments, along with Marxist authority, have universally sought to use language and image to bring disgrace to material reality, along with psychological humiliation and subservience to the lives of the vast majority of their respective citizens. Such questions, they sniff, are not fit subjects for literature.

They do not (as Borges must have occasionally done despite his numerous and invariably coy protestations that he was innocent of all worldly knowledge) operate in self-conscious defiance of political authority. For them, authority is simply part of their inherited data field – no more and no less important than, say, the mannerist novels of Jane Austen or the surrealisms of Garcia Marquez – and considerably less important than the Volvo stationwagons in their driveways. When they try to write literature themselves, and if they get beyond the vapid testimonies to how sensitive and erudite they are, they tend to go the Borges route, building rhetorical palaces for the elusive and the perverse. The best of them are masters at taming these to walk on leashes into mystified irrelevance. Eric McCormack seems typical of this latter kind of academic writer, one who has emerged from the English department corridors with full technical mastery of this minor intellectual enterprise.

Which brings us to Garcia Marquez, who is the joker in the deck who reveals, by accident, the contradictions inherent in McCormack's methodology. In the last thirty years, Latin America has emerged (for those who want to recognize it) as the political dark cellar of Western democracy. In most South and Central American republics, the official institutions are similar to those in the functioning northern states, but there the resemblance ends. As we have seen in various violent episodes in Chile, Argentina, Brazil and across Central America, their institutions are riddled with corruption, and behind the eggshell-thin facades, brutal authority is eminently willing to expose its violence and its grinning arbitrariness.

For Latin American artists of all kinds, surrealism satisfies the craving for liberty of expression while still holding some small guarantees – because its maniacal energies are persuasive and symbolic rather than confrontational – that an artist attempting to reveal truth will have a chance of eluding the terrors of authority, with its willingness to transgress constitutional guarantees with torture or with the disappearing of the author or members of his or her family.

Yet like the European surrealism of the 1920s, Latin American surrealism – or magic realism, as it is now called – is also a structural expression of bewilderment over the gulf between constitutional (or official) and received reality. As such, it often takes expression as a formalist protest against a parallel gulf between the rhetoric of social and political structures and personal experience. But unlike its European cousin, the Latin American practice of surrealism manipulates some well-known patterns of authoritarian behaviour at dangerously close range. The chief is that government-sanctioned torturers and killers are more likely to punish moral abrasiveness than sensual obtuseness and/or kinkiness. One can imagine an Argentine or Chilean or Salvadoran military officer jerking off between prisoner interrogations over the desecration of the virgin Erendira in *One Hundred Years of Solitude*.

The imitation of this kind of writing by safe, well-educated, university-based academic fiction writers is peculiar, to say the least. After all, these ninnies have nothing in their lives that requires the protective cover of surrealist behaviour. No one is going to disappear them or their loved ones, and the only form of harassment they are likely to be subjected to is an occasional disgruntled student letting the air from the tires of their family stationwagons. They're magic realists without any respect for magic or reality, or better, they're postmodernists without any understanding of the sources of postmodernism or what it is doing in other disciplines.

Their attraction to Borges, Kafka and even to Garcia Marquez lies in the ostensible perverse obstinacy that is central to the intellectual method of all three. In the case of Borges, who was bookish and intellectual in the face of a political and social milieu that held his political disinterestedness and his library in even greater contempt than contemporary North American society does, they see an heroic rationale for their own apoliticality of thought and living habits. Nowhere in our civilization does one hear more talk of government conspiracies to remove or sully individual rights than among these writers as they patrol the office corridors of the literature departments. And nowhere are there more bullshit-laden structures to ensure continued job security and work privileges than can be found in contemporary university tenure agreements.

They regard Garcia Marquez – quite accurately – as a political trickster who has avoided all the authoritarian pitfalls of his culture. Tricksters, remember, were very much in vogue during the 1960s and early 70s when most of these people were still students or junior faculty. In him they see another salutary role model, despite the fact that the cultural differences between Garcia Marquez's milieu and their own are such that the relative dangers of producing highly sym-bolized surrealist literature are equivalent to one man swimming across the piranha-infested Amazon and another crossing a bathtub filled with Mr. Bubble.

One supposes that in Kafka they see yet another kindred spirit. Deifying Borges and Garcia Marquez is a self-serving co-option of writers who only make sense in an atmosphere of direct political vio-lence and mediocrity. One can admire the cunning of it, or one can sneer at its intellectual foolishness. But the co-option of the imagi-nation of Franz Kafka is more offensive. Kafka's vision has been so disturbingly accurate about the mechanics of this civilization that it has been suppressed to the point where it – and Kafka, who was a deeply private and subtle man – have become little more than a Dis-neyfied adjective.

What a shame. Kafka's imagination of the world effectively argues against the delusion of the ascendancy of personality, privacy and individuality. Moreover, Kafka is profoundly instructive con-cerning the methods authority has at its disposal to undermine the individual. In a way, these magic realist/postmodernist nitwits have anaesthetized and depoliticized Kafka, treating his vision either as a riskless aesthetic strategy or as science fiction.

Now, I know it has become fashionable to go around accusing people of being postmodern without being clear what postmodern-ism is. So I'm going to stop ranting about academic nitwits and nin-nies and give you my definition of postmodernism. Then I'm going to go back and apply it to Eric McCormack.

Postmodernism really began as a reaction to the narrowness with which modernism defined human function and utility. In architec-ture, where the results of ideas have physical dimensions, modernism gave us slab architecture – those sealed-system monoliths that were supposed to make people work efficiently – and which a lot of workers are currently discovering are uninhabitable. In literature, modernism gave us Ezra Pound and his lunatic fascism. Modernism is technocratic, class-bound, and authoritarian.

Postmodernism is different only in its distaste for modernist images of authoritarian utility. If anything, it is more technocratic and class-bound than modernism. And because it is purely a reaction to modernism, it rarely does more than flip all the surface values. Hence, postmodern architecture is at best a series of titillatingly anti-functionalist historical quotes. At worst, it is bric-a-brac and plaster facades that soften the surface impact of slab modernism without challenging it in any serious structural way.

Literary postmodernism is similar. At its best, it is a series of quotes – often direct ones of technique or subject matter – from what is regarded as a tradition that has become at once historical and simultaneous. At its worst, it is simple middle-class onanism – pornography for the impotent, or a kind of low-grade cultural cocaine to compete politely with the high-grade stuff coming out of Global Village television and motion picture conduits. It sets your teeth on edge, like the other stuff, but it's dead easy to walk away from.

Why bring cocaine into this? Well, cocaine distorts perception in predictable ways, remember. The ground for sensation is heightened along with that of the self. What is diminished by that narrow enhancement is invariably the world, which becomes a mere projection of the ego and the raw material of sensation. Cokeheads are prone to mistake difficulty for conspiracy and moral complexity for evil incarnate, and after a while (shortly before the nasal tissue atrophies or an overdose explodes the brain) the impulse to amuse the self *becomes* the self. That pretty much describes the writing of Eric McCormack and the work of much of the leading edge of postmodernism.

Postmodernists believe that as a progressive and/or deterministic force, history has ended, and that all technology and content is therefore contemporary. Hence, postmodernism is relativistic, pluralist, experiential, unmoral, and deliberately idiosyncratic. Style, novelty and process are everything, sort of like they are in a shopping mall.

In Eric McCormack's *Inspecting the Vaults* one can see postmodernism operating in full flight, as it were. In it, history has been utterly supplanted by anecdote and idiosyncrasy. In one story, for instance, Leon Trotsky is treated not as a man who changed the world (and was indirectly or directly responsible for millions of deaths) but as someone who was accidentally photographed by the friend of a friend as he was pulled off a boat on Canada's east coast. Such a view isn't accidental at all.

Take a closer look at the title story. The conceit the story uses is an authoritarian structure – in this instance a fanciful prison complex consisting of units of seven houses, six of them inhabited by citizens who keep prisoners in vaults beneath the houses. The seventh house, which has no basement, is the residence of the "inspector", the narrator. This man goes out monthly to inspect the vaults and their prisoners, thence to report on conditions to the unexplained central "authority" of the story (I will leave that irony alone).

What follows, not surprisingly, is a catalog of the various inhabitants of the vaults. The catalog is a series of anecdotes of gratuitous gore, kinky sex, and what I suppose is called, in Borgesian circles, "imaginations" – lists of odd inventions, people carrying out logical extensions of unexamined and irrational premises, and the like.

In one of McCormack's vaults is the inventor of a horde of quasi-mechanical forest animals who inhabited a synthetic forest constructed over centuries by the inventor's ancestors. The inventor has been imprisoned for resisting the extermination of his creations. Another vault contains a more sadistic inventor, this time of mechanical contraptions that poison, torture and kill people and animals. A third cell contains a young, sexually alluring (but only for those who associate sexual pleasure with death, torture and vomit) woman who instantly exposes "her full breasts and her dark sex" to the reader, and appears to be a cross between a siren and Linda Blair from *The Exorcist*. Dragged before a magistrate on a charge of witchcraft (the narrator tells us), she vomited up the following list of items:

> ...four moray eels, each one a foot-and-a-half long; seven hanks of wool, all the colours of the rainbow, braided together like intertwined snakes; a bone-handled carving knife; a loaded .44 automatic pistol; a dozen compacted balls of cat and dog hair, mainly ginger and black; three engraved granite rocks, each six inches in diameter (she heaved them up, they say, like a snake regurgitating eggs); an unknown quantity of dung of such animals as cows, horses, and rabbits; countless pints of blood, not her own type, according to pathologists; a book written in a language experts have not yet been able to identify; and a parchment that contained a detailed description of this very encounter with the elderly magistrate – had he chosen to pick it up and read it as soon as she vomited it up, tragedy might have been averted. He chose not to, which the parchment had foretold.

Now isn't that a great list? Didn't you just *love* the Borgesian twist about the parchment? The tragedy that could have been averted, if you're still interested, was that several sentences later the woman pulled the .44 from the barf pile and shot the magistrate in the stomach (sorry, we don't find out if he died). I mean, like, wow!

This narration trails its indignities to the human spirit across seventeen gore-streaked pages, and includes a really charming anecdote about the reason for the inspector's incarceration – the authorities found the tattooed and tanned shell of a young woman buried in his garden.

Now, my assumption is that Mr. McCormack is gesturing in all this about the arbitrary nature of human authority and of the individual and collective behaviour of human beings and nature as they are enfolded by or collide with that authority. But what is totally absent in his gestures is any understanding that in the world outside his fictions authority may appear to be arbitrary, but it is sure as hell not an irrational invention. The logic and goals of the world we live in may be insane, but they are always logical, and they are ultimately traceable. I happen to think it is the job of literature to trace that logic and to unmask its insane goals. What my own investigations have discovered so far convinces me that they are never as glamourous or dramatic as they are in McCormack's fanciful situations.

I could offer up innumerable examples of McCormack's deranged cynicisms and surrealisms from other stories in the book. I won't, because to do so would be to spread the infection. Suffice it to say that a startling number of animals get dismembered in this book, and that women are singled out for particularly brutal treatment, much of it anally targeted. I don't want to seem even more protestant than I am, and I'm fully aware that Sophocles didn't have to fuck his mother to write *Oedipus Rex*. Even so, maybe we really are responsible for what we think about.

Aside from his own peculiar imaginative lights, McCormack's frame of reference is primarily other writers and writing styles, with a little obligatory Canadiana thrown in to hook colleagues selecting new books for their local literature courses. When he isn't swinging a meat cleaver at some innocent imaginary victim, he's quoting from the intellectual repertoires and idiosyncrasies of other writers, without feeling the need to grapple with the realities they may have faced. Kafka and Garcia Marquez faced their respective worlds. There is evidence to suggest that Borges at least knew that one was out there. McCormack demonstrably doesn't give a shit if it is there or not. He's a "creative" writer, so besotted by his postmodernist elan – and his academic security – that he is content to jerk human reality around by whichever appendage he can get hold of.

I'm not criticizing McCormack or writers like him for their anti-ideological stance. I'd be the first to agree that art and ideology run contradictory programs. What I'm saying is almost the opposite: that their lack of any detectable interest in questions related to authority hides an extremely reactionary (if covert) ideological stance, a demand (or wish) that the present structure of privilege and rewards be allowed to exist unexamined. They want to go on creating morally opaque sensory experiences, because that is the privilege accorded them by the existing forms of authority, and allows them to think of themselves as artists. What I object to, and loudly, is that they think their status as artists legitimizes the other unexamined privileges they accept. It doesn't.

Given all this, what does Eric McCormack's *Inspecting the Vaults* mean? Well, on its own narrow terms, very damned little. It's light entertainment for those with an off-colour sense of humour, a third-rate exhibition of contemporary conventional literary skills. For Canada, however, it is a minor milestone. Alice Munro has proved that Canadian writers can master modernist fiction, and I suppose McCormack demonstrates that we've now mastered postmodernist fiction, such as it is.

On second thought, however, perhaps it may contain a more profound message, something beyond sex, drugs and rock & roll. Maybe it is telling us that it's time we all moved on to something I'll call neomodernism.

Neomodernism is not yet a movement, but one can see it stirring in the debris and carnage of postmodern architecture. By the time it arrives it will no doubt have a different name, but it will have characteristics that address the shortcomings of both modernism and postmodernism. Instead of merely reacting to the authoritarian definitions of social function and utility inherent in modernism, as architectural postmodernism has done, neomodernism would raise a frontal challenge to those ugly definitions of authority and function – by returning to ask fundamental questions about why things are built, and for whose benefit.

A neomodernist literature could go even further. It would return to the fundamental (and absurd) questions of existence: Why are we alive? What is the responsibility of the individual toward others (or of the function-group to the body politic)? What limitations should be placed on authority? What new forms of creeping authority need to be unmasked and exposed? What is the nature and purpose of the human community, and what place (if any) does art and artifice have in its maintenance, manipulation and/or survival? Neomodern literature would ask all the same questions, plus at least one additional one: What is literature for?

Those are nasty questions. But if we don't get onto answering them soon, there will be no more literature, no more stationwagons, and no more leisure for people like Eric McCormack to write books.

Carry on Bumping

DAVID McFADDEN'S DILEMMAS

A while back I was lucky enough to get to a private screening of a very funny film based on David McFadden's *A Trip Around Lake Ontario*. The first two volumes of this five-volume set of travel books, *A Trip Around Lake Huron* and *A Trip Around Lake Erie*, were published by Coach House, sort of, several years ago, and the three books, together or separate, are among the funniest and best books published in this country in the last thirty years. They have also received amazingly little critical attention or public circulation.

In one of the sequences in the Lake Ontario film, McFadden is walking along a storm-battered concrete seawall. It is a typical McFadden tableau: he is lonely as a cloud, and the voice-over narrator – McFadden himself – is telling you why he is bereft. He is lamenting his estranged wife and children, bemoaning his outcast fate and his fall from domestic grace. Then, at the crucial moment of the film sequence, McFadden actually does fall, not from grace but from the seawall. I'm pretty sure he didn't plan either fall. I'm not certain what caused his real-life fall because writers always lie about their personal lives, but in the film, he simply skidded off the rough concrete seawall and disappeared behind it. The awkwardness (in both cases) lets you know he's hurt himself. You're concerned for him, but you're also helpless with laughter.

Saying that the film sequence is in the same league with Chaplin and Buster Keaton is only a slight exaggeration. After all, McFadden's filmic pratfall wasn't planned. But saying that it is at least ten times funnier than anything Wayne and Shuster ever accomplished isn't an exaggeration at all. Yet at the same time, none of the comparisons quite work, just as none of the Trips books can be compared with real life, or with any comedic writing I know of. McFadden's humour is unique. It's always slightly unsettling, and at times it can become distinctly unpleasant.

The film has been recut on video, but you're not likely to see it on television. The Canadian Broadcasting Corporation was interested in it for a while, but they wanted to cut out a couple of typical McFadden sequences that they think are a bit too off-colour for Canadian audiences. The sequences happen to be set in a stripper bar, but the reasons for wanting them out don't have anything to do with bared breasts or lust or even lurid language. In them, McFadden is talking to the strippers, and his voice-over is describing the strippers' love of, and hard luck with, their pets. One of them, he reports, had a budgie, but it flew into a pan of boiling water. Another stripper lost four guinea pigs to an unknown assailant who murdered them and left them on the back step with their internal organs removed. It's funny, but it's also unsettling. Consequently the biggest joke in the film is the usual one. It's on McFadden. Few people will get to see the video unless they watch Sunday morning cultural programming on television, or hang out in the depths of Toronto's avant-garde arts community.

All three Trips books are loaded with the same kind of bizarre slapstick and disjunction. The slapstick is lightning quick and universal, a product of McFadden's directness of perception and the ordinariness of the human situations he depicts. Yet for all the ordinariness of those situations, his subject matter is rarely trivial or sentimental, and in the tradition of great comedy, there are dark pools lurking in most episodes. McFadden knows that the conventional realities we take for granted are eggshell thin and he breaks the shell constantly to reveal what they hide. Or maybe they break because he's inadvertently stumbled against them when he really wanted to tiptoe past. With him, you're never sure.

Any of dozens of episodes from the Trips books could illustrate what I'm getting at. For instance, in another episode, this time from *A Trip Around Lake Huron*, McFadden runs afoul of some mushrooms. Throughout the book he's been mildly preoccuppied with mushrooms – edible wild mushrooms, psychedelic mushrooms, poisonous mushrooms. Because he is never quite sure of anything, he's never sure whether the mushrooms he finds are edible. Finally he eats twelve mushrooms he is "almost totally certain" are *Amanita frostiana*, a mushroom identified by his manual as "probably edible". He tries to get his wife and kids to eat them with him, but they decline. He eats them alone, and on the sly.

The mushrooms turn out to be poisonous, but McFadden can't admit it to his family because he's tried to get them to eat them. His wife refused on safety grounds, chiding him for wanting to put his loved ones in jeopardy to satisfy his evidently chronic obsessive curiosity. Absurdly, but with characteristic logic, he takes his family to a movie that same evening, convinced that he's going to die of mushroom poisoning but unable to tell them because he can't bear to face their contempt for his having tried to poison them along with himself. Then, after puking violently in the theatre washroom, and lying to his wife about it, he realizes that the mushrooms are also psychotropic, and he proceeds to enjoy the new sensations, even though he thinks he's going to die any minute.

When I first read this episode I was embarrassed that I found it so funny, and disturbed that I couldn't quite forget about it. I knew I'd survived similar episodes myself, but writing so clearly about it requires a different kind of skill and courage than I have. Since I'm normal enough to dislike being embarrassed and disturbed, I tried to figure out what it was in the episode that made me feel as I did.

Part of it had to do with the relationship between McFadden the character in a book, and McFadden the writer. McFadden-the-character – in the Trips books, anyway – is the ultimate straight man, a person who believes in democratic institutions and in the essential benevolence of an information-rich civilization in which no accurate, detailed information – on either people or things – is available or exchangeable. That's why he eats poisonous mushrooms and then isn't able to ask the people he loves for help or understanding. McFadden-the-writer understands this contradiction perfectly.

So are the two McFaddens the same man? He doesn't say. He isn't crazy, or if he is, he's wise-crazy enough to refuse arbitrary resolutions to these kinds of contradictions. I happen to believe he's perfectly sane, and that the world is crazy. And that is a strange and disturbing thought.

I'll tell you what else I believe about this man. In almost any other country in which unprogrammed laughter is permitted (and that is a constantly shrinking list), David McFadden would be treated as a national treasure. But in Canada he is being ignored by the press and media, and he is bullied or tricked into being a purely literary writer by more aggressive or corrupt contemporaries. Academic critics are merely confused by him, as they are with any large, unconventional intelligence.

McFadden calls himself a poet, an academic designation that is as common as ratshit in this country, and about as cherished. Unquestionably, McFadden is a poet, but in the same way Aristophanes was, or Jonathan Swift. As a thinking poet – rare these days – his closest ties are to Baudelaire and the Japanese Haiku artists. He has fine skills, but not commercial ones. The skills that could bring him public acclaim are his skills as a humourist, and with these, he has no parallel I've ever encountered.

McFadden's comic gifts aren't recognized, except by the small coterie of readers who search out his books because Canada's cultural establishment, with its tourist-bureau mentality, has arrested our public concept of humour somewhere in the early part of the century. We are unable to move beyond the colonial humour of Stephen Leacock, and we are encouraged to be amused only by the sophomoric or the parochial. Our officially sanctioned humourists – Wayne and Shuster and journalists like Allan Fotheringham – plunder our sensibilities with in-jokes that contain no venom, vulgar set-jokes and slapstick that have all the comic timing of a herd of cows cropping a meadow. The laughter they evoke is self-satisfied and exclusionary. If you already know the joke, you can laugh. If you don't, you're probably from Timmins or North Battleford or Dawson Creek. Chances are, you're the butt of the joke.

McFadden's humour isn't like that. He observes the rules of the modern world by turning its rulebook inside out: Anything can happen, and anything can be mistaken for evil monstrousness. Kindness, innocence or virtue are no defence against anything. His humour is always loaded. However hard you find yourself laughing, you're always implicated by it. It makes you uneasy. What McFadden practises, as announced by his 1984 collection of "poems", is the art of darkness.

When the first two Trips books were sent to the Leacock Awards Committee, they were returned, I've been told, with a note saying "send us something that's funny." The cultural establishment in this country doesn't like dark laughter, not unless one can feel the cords tying it to Northrop Frye, Leacock, or somebody at CBC with a budget and a house in Rosedale.

Aside from a rare ability to write direct, clear English sentences, McFadden's governing gifts are as simple as his execution of them is deft. He has an extraordinarily – and I suspect involuntarily – direct and immediate field of focus. Guiding this gift is a second one – he is a compulsive logician.

The first time I met McFadden, he related a story to me about a recent trip he'd made to the Shaw Festival. He'd obtained front-row tickets so he could watch the actors at close quarters, something I've learned he likes to do with pretty well everything he does. I expected a critique of the play, but the play wasn't what had received his primary attention. The performance, he said, was magnificent, although he couldn't quite remember which play he'd seen. What he saw instead was that the actors on stage kept spitting on one another. One actress, he said gleefully, took a major shot right in the eye without flinching or losing her lines. Amazing powers of short-term concentration, he added, shaking his head with obvious pleasure at the memory. Amazing.

Amazing powers of concentration are also precisely what he has. What he sees in everything is not what is intended or what is being projected, but the slapstick that resides just beneath conventional perceptual and cultural facades, and only becomes visible when the direct phenomena are the primary focus.

McFadden also has the audacity to follow whatever immediate logic a situation presents to his receptors. In one poem, a young medical student brings the cadavers of dead children home to "practise on" in his spare time. Cadavers of children are conveniently small, and the chief problem is therefore not the expected moral one, but the practical one of getting them through the streets undetected. And of course, his character loses one. In another poem, a cow breaks out of a slaughter house and swims Lake Ontario. It *has* to swim the lake because that's the only way it can possibly escape. Logical as hell, as everything is in McFadden's tales. And if it's a slightly crazy world he depicts, remember that the one we accept as normal is a whole lot crazier when *its* logical premises are challenged.

Notwithstanding the "who's the crazy one" argument, such an idiosyncratic view of reality as McFadden's is bound to be perverse and dark. It contains no ready access to the common illusions that keep most of us from having to admit that the world we're in, with its 20,000-plus nuclear warheads, is becoming – or has become – a vast lunatic fringe surrounding solipsistic logic systems our institutions and leaders worship but don't control. McFadden's method is Don

Quixote's method: the logic of the cosmically near-sighted. McFadden makes few bones about the way reality works. He's too busy parodying it. And remember that in Don Quixote, the windmills attacked as monsters frequently turn out to be monsters.

So what is McFadden's dilemma? There are several. McFadden's first dilemma is that his books are not being read. That is a function of at least two different distinctly Canadian phenomena.

1. Lack of distribution. McFadden has had a long association with two of Canada's most successful author-killing presses: Coach House and McClelland & Stewart. In the past, Coach House has killed authors by not distributing the books they print so elegantly. Sure, Coach House is an author-run press that has done pioneer work in the computerization of Canadian publishing, and it has published some very beautiful books, and some very good ones. Actually, nearly everyone I've met from Coach House is incredibly decent and well-meaning. More than that, they're competent at what they do, and they do it with a refreshing absence of professionalist hype. But the pioneer days in Canada are over, even in the cultural community. We have a national culture. It has been around long enough for it to have produced its own class system, with its ruling classes in the universities and a vast and increasingly marginalized underclass who are expected to feel so grateful at getting a book into print or a play onto a stage that they don't care that no one reads their books or comes to see their plays.

If I were more cynical I'd suggest that the Coach House problem exists because the majority on the editorial board can't believe that all Canadian writers don't make at least $40,000 a year teaching in colleges and universities, but I think it's actually more complicated than that. Partly it is the result of a system in which most of Canada's influential older writers are attached to universities and are party to the BMW / high income / literature-as-curriculum-vitae-protection syndrome. Another part of it can be accounted to pretty much what Robin Mathews says is the problem with Canadian culture in general: that we have a built-in inferiority complex. And partly, it is the very real problem of working with a numerically small and geographically dispersed market that is in direct competition with the most powerful cultural apparatus in world history.

Coach House, like most small presses, supports writers, but not economically. Even for writers who don't need the income (McFadden does), cultural gratification without economic gratification becomes toxic. Their time gets taken up by other things, and their ability to imagine a public culture disintegrates. Most of them eventually become rancorous amateurs.

McClelland & Stewart is actually more author-toxic to literary writers than Coach House, but the toxicity is more subtle. They have the apparatus to distribute books, but they don't use it. They operate out of a two-tier system of publishing, in which they hold a prestigious list of literary authors like McFadden and others who they use to legitimize their claim to being Canada's first and best press. The other tier in the system consists of the people M&S think of as commercial authors, to whom they accord the real benefits of big-press distribution and publicity.

Ironically, McFadden publishes his potentially "commercial" books, such as the Trips books, with Coach House, and publishes his major poetry collections, which have a much smaller chance of gaining a large audience, with M&S. Meanwhile, to make a living, he sits on the Coach House editorial board, and does typesetting for them. He also edits books for a variety of presses. It's a tricky situation to be in. Even if he wants to, McFadden, like anybody in that situation, will think twice before aiming a hard kick at either press, because they're his friends and sometimes his employers.

2. McFadden's second dilemma is self-definition. This is probably the only country in the world in which poets of working-class descent and outlook expect to earn a middle-class income from writing poetry. It's a very common aberration, and it doesn't seem to matter that not one single one of them has been able to make a decent living from poetry. What is bizarre is that most of them ascribe the

lack of income to a fault in themselves, not in the cultural system or in their expectations. They just don't figure it out. Maybe it's because poetry is an avocation, and like all such tremolos in the sociopolitical structure, the zone of practical interface between reality and expectation is invisible to the victims. Let's not kid ourselves: poetry in Canada is the avocation of professional teachers, the independently wealthy, and quite frequently, of idiots. McFadden is none of those, least of all an idiot. But he's still a victim of his own self-definition.

McFadden's personal background is a rather unusual one for a poet. His ancestors were Irish hobbits, and he comes from a socially conservative working-class background. Until 1976 McFadden lived a kind of Walter Mitty existence in Hamilton, Ontario, working as a newspaper reporter and writing in his spare time. Since 1976 he's worked at a variety of economically marginal writing jobs – writer-in-residence at various institutions, and as a freelance editor, typesetter and proofreader – jobs that have allowed him more time to write. Since he doesn't have any university degrees, he can't, as most of his friends do, make a comfortable and secure living from the universities.

In a sociological sense, the result is an anomaly – a peculiarly Canadian one. McFadden thinks of himself as a poet, and evidently makes his fundamental literary, intellectual and publishing decisions on that basis. Yet the intellectual tools he posesses, and his writing skills, are well beyond those of most of his contemporaries. What's peculiarly Canadian about this is that his background, sensibility and economic prospects don't provide him with any of the privileges historically accorded to poets.

What's painful about it is that McFadden is a poet, and a gifted one. His *Gypsy Guitar* (1987) is the best volume of verse published in Canada during the 1980s, and the only one that most people read in 50-page gulps. The literary model for the poems is Baudelaire, and the subject matter is perversity, McFadden style. I'm not in total agreement with what it has to say about gypsies or guitars, because

McFadden is no gypsy, and the energies in the poems don't resemble the sentimental syrup usually associated with gypsy guitar music. That's part of the dilemma, too: a determinedly anti-commercial title from a writer who needs and deserves commercial success.

All this leads to McFadden's third dilemma. What kind of writer does he have to become in order to have his work more widely read? First, given his lack of university degrees and a temperament and creative energies that make it a personal agony that he does not have the economic leeway to pursue his own projects full-time, he has no literary alternative but to become a commercially successful writer.

Just for fun, are there other alternatives? Could he take up another line of work and become a private poet, leaving the judgment and distribution of his work to future generations? I try to imagine him as a lawyer, but his deviousness is all wrong for that. Police work might be okay. After all, most writers have a peculiar relationship with authority. Kierkegaard once remarked that if he couldn't be a writer he would have preferred to be an agent for the secret police. That's an amusing thought, but it wouldn't work with McFadden. He's too anarchistic, and combined with his mildly paranoiac personality and his gift for anecdotal thinking, he'd either become a new kind of Inspector Clousseau, or he'd wind up in the control rooms of NATO. It's safer for everyone if he remains a writer. He's told me that he'd be happy driving a taxi, but having driven in a car with him a couple of times, I don't think the taxi companies (or the public) would appreciate him very much this way.

McFadden should be making a decent living as a writer. But what kind of writer? He would make a marvellous newspaper or magazine columnist. Or he could be a sports writer. Or a remote zen psychoanalyst, administering koan and haiku therapy to the intellectually needy. He could be any of those because he writes clear simple sentences compulsively, whether he's describing a bird he just saw fly into a pot of boiling water, or discussing Being and Nothingness, both of which he's capable of summarizing in a single paragraph.

But if someone offered him such jobs, I doubt if he'd take them. Against all the evidence that tells him that it isn't economically possible, he still wants to be known as a poet, or at least as a literary author.

The only purely literary writers in this era who come close to making their living from writing are novelists. Even then, they make most of it from selling the movie and television rights to their work. McFadden isn't a novelist. A man who believes that the continuities and transitions in human reality are governed or set off by coincidence – as McFadden professes is the case – should not write novels.

If you don't believe me, read his novel, *Canadian Sunset*. It's his first attempt to write a conventional novel, and it's a very strange book. Read in small parcels, it's rife with McFadden magic: small underminings of normality, coincidences, people having conversations about weird subjects in conventional settings. But if you scope back a little, everything in the book is slightly off-kilter. The coincidences pile onto one another, and there are no secure motivations for the characters doing what they do, saying what they say, acting out what they act out. It's as if he took a string of perceptual anecdotes or a book of poems and ran them through a blender so they'd all have the texture of conventional literary narrative. They do, and at the same time, they're bubbling with McFadden's arealities.

The book doesn't demean McFadden's talent. But it is like watching Wayne Gretzky play goalie, or Andre Dawson trying be a catcher, or Erik Satie writing a symphony for accordion. Novelists are puppeteers, and they work with all kinds of rhetorical props about "human nature" and individual character that aren't natural to McFadden. The result is a novel that isn't going to be bought up for the movies, and probably won't be read beyond McFadden's existing readership.

That leads us to McFadden's fourth dilemma. It's a dilemma that faces pretty well every writer in Canada who isn't content with the shrinking community of citizens who value and read literature. The dilemma is this: what can individual writers do about the specific problem of the disappearance of literature's public audience, and the replacement of that audience by a privileged and professional audience?

Even to confront this dilemma properly, one must recognize its place in the larger context it is rooted in: the cultural atomization that is going on across Western civilization and particularly in English-speaking North America. We are all being subjected to a systematic but non-conspiratorial program aimed at destroying public discourse. This program is being carried out by decultured business visigoths who have no notion of the categorical imperative-based social contract each citizen is supposed to make with the body politic.

The entrepreneurial elan of current political and economic practices operates in total ignorance of that root. It does not deny it or argue for opposed values. If it did, discourse would ensue, and we would be back in a game that could at least be won or lost, on merit. But the post-war era has operated, without a formal declaration, on the dual bases of self-aggrandizing subjectivity and expedience. The economic system has slowly subsumed our political and moral systems, both of which have been retooled as subsidiary support structures to consumerism. In a sense, we have been taken over by a barbarian culture without noticing it has happened.

Canadian literary writers making an honest attempt to locate their audience will be forced to admit that they no longer have a direct one. Instead, they have a market. The cultural market is structured like most contemporary consumer markets, albeit with a difference: it bypasses the general public. The writers are the manufacturers, farmers, resource extractors. The wholesale intermediaries – the English departments of our colleges and universities – pass the product off to the retailers – which in reality is the government. And since the government really doesn't require a physical product, but rather a "culture" or a "national identity", the literary writers are alone in wanting to actually see their books being read by the public. The wholesalers and retailers are satisfied with things as they are. Why not? *They* get paid.

One defence that I've heard some writers make of this system is that "serious literature" bears the same relationship to public culture as the arms race does to consumer technology. They argue that it's a variation of the "technological spinoff" argument. Down the line, the spinoff argument goes, the advances made by the military went into the space program, and that in turn led to civil applications and a new generation of consumer products that have transformed civil life. Certainly it is true that the techniques of, say, Imagism, along with Reich and Jung's discoveries about the structure of mass human consciousness, are being beamed at us now in the form of television commercials and other forms of consumer manipulation. But public discourse and critical consciousness rarely lend themselves to economic expedience, and given the barbarian nature of the new power structure, will probably be replaced by something more easily managed when and if they interfere too much with the commodity jamboree. Nobody up there – or is it *down there*? – loves artists, and it's time we woke up to the implications of that.

I don't think the old truisms about accepting obscurity as the price of being a serious artist and letting the future take care of public distribution can stand up under scrutiny much longer, either. We're living in a culture that, intentionally or not, is headed toward the extermination of public discourse and private imagination, and toward the integration of ideas and intellect into an utterly relativistic market economy.

I happen to have a background as an urban planner, and perhaps it has given me a weakness for the concept of "highest and best use of urban amenities." McFadden, it seems to me, is an urban amenity who is being grossly misused and/or underused. He needs to rethink what he's doing, and with whom he does it. And we need to be generous enough, and far-sightedly insistent enough, to help him get the public audience he deserves, even if it means tearing down the system of privileges that is backhanding literature into the dumper.

Books in Canada

THE POET'S WORK

I've lived in Vancouver for almost 25 years. For most of that time I called myself a poet. Even though I still practise the craft of poetry as seriously as I ever did, my business card now reads simply, "writer". But I still live and work in a subculture where poets are common, and I've talked, played and fought with hundreds of other poets of varying seriousness and skill over the years. If this all sounds like the preamble to another joke about the overabundance of poets in Canada, you can relax. That's not quite what this is about.

During my years in Vancouver, I encountered just one poet who works at his craft day in and day out. No, I'm not that person. For most of the years when I called myself a poet, I operated, as most poets seem to, on the principle that not having to labour at my craft was one of the employment benefits of the job. It was the laboratory, to use T.S. Eliot's phrase, that held the fascination for me, not the work. I enjoyed hanging around poets and their metaphors, and I enjoyed compiling the raw data for poetry, but it didn't occur to me that processing the data should be a matter of habitual, backbreaking labour. I thought composition was a mystical activity, and I had to be shown, by another poet, that such is not the case. Poets have to work, like anyone else. And their labours are no easier than those of any other artisan.

The poet who taught me this is Norm Sibum. For more than a decade now, Sibum has lived on Commercial Drive, driven taxi, and worked on his poetry daily. He has worked on a single volume of poems, and for those who are interested, sections of it have been released as extremely obscure chapbooks: *Small Commerce* (1979, by Caitlin Press) and *Among Other Howls in the Storm* (1982, from Pulp Press) come to mind. More recently, Sibum has allowed an antiquarian bookseller named William Hoffer to letterpress two more chapbooks. One is a ten-poem section from the book, the other contains eight more. They're available under the informative titles of *Ten Poems* and *Eight Poems* – both for the ludicrous price of $75. Both chapbooks are elegantly printed, but unless you're a print fetishist, they're not quite worth the admission price. Oberon Press has also published two collections, one of which is a typical Oberon production with an uncorrected American lexicon and no title on the cover. But neither the price of chapbooks nor the incompetence of Canada's cherished small presses is what this is about, although both are tempting targets.

At any given time, Sibum's book – still untitled – consists of between 40 and 70 pages of verse, always in exact measure to the current state of his understanding of his street, of the poetic measure of its economy, social life, and historical implications, and to his command of the instructions of an exceedingly demanding muse. I've known him personally for much of the time he's been working on it, but only for a period of three or four years was I close to his work, to his obscure fidelities, and to his rigorous methods of composition.

I could go the usual route from here and talk about his personal eccentricities, which are legion and not always attractive. Like most obsessive people, Sibum is not the most pleasant person in the world. He's neurotically grumpy about the future and the condition of poetry, and socially he can be a terrible mixer who finds it irresistible to inveigle himself between any two serious long-term combatants he can locate. As a result, he does not keep friends for very long. On the lighter side, he retains, in his mid-40s, a perfect ego as an athlete, be it for baseball, volleyball, basketball or pool, each of which he plays as if they were forms of solitaire, part of his habitual outward gloominess. I could talk about his unusual baseball batting stance, which is so relaxed that opposing pitchers frequently ask him if he is ready. I could also talk about his background as an exile and draft dodger, his early life as a U.S. Army brat, or about his endless insecurities about having so small an audience for his work. But to discuss him in any of these ways would be to ignore the essential piece of information about him: that his personality and his private identity are secondary to his commitment to his Muse, and to the operation of his craft.

His untitled volume is not yet Great Poetry. Dennis Lee, who recognized the depth and seriousness of Sibum's undertaking, rejected versions of poems from the book for inclusion into the M&S anthology of Canadian poets of the 1970s and 80s. Lee rejected the poems with all the agonized moral contortions one expects of an intelligent man thrusting his foot down his own throat, having been trained, in the bizarre commercial aesthetics of CanLit, to recognize superior publication value in the narrowly conceived and executed confessional poems of people like Roo Borson, Roo Di Cicco, Roo Di Michele and (come to think of it) me. What measures Lee's error – and his anthology – is that by the time the rejection landed in Sibum's lap, the versions of the poems Lee had rejected had been revised eight or nine times and most had been pushed out of the ever-changing compositional frame of the book. Sibum was stung, but he couldn't quite remember which versions he'd sent to Lee.

I've seen as many as thirty revisions of a single Sibum poem, and the revisions are never cursory alterations of a few ill-placed words.

Each time a poem gets redone, it is turned end over end, pulled apart, re-researched, written out by hand, corrected again and then re-typed. For the revision of three or four poems he was working on at the same time, I've watched him ransack a good portion of Roman history and literature, looking for the truth of a casual line in Virgil that called into question the accuracy of Sibum's working structure: something that the Muse whispered.

In one recent revision, it was a conversation between St. Augustine and his mother about imagining the voice of God without access to the singing of birds, the caress of the breeze along the leaftips of the boulevard trees. For that he read a large portion of the canon of Medieval theology, while across the street from the second floor tenement window that allows him to write and observe the streetscape at the same time, kids were breaking windows on a block of abandoned shops awaiting redevelopment. One of the shops was the old campaign office of an unsuccessful right-wing politician. Another was called, cryptically, "The Third World". It all got into the revisions.

Watching Sibum's book progress is at once sobering and uplifting. The illusions most poets carry about their importance to this particular human civilization are exposed in their futility and self-aggrandizing arrogance by his method. He risks his entire understanding with every line, and frequently, that understanding fails. When it does, he quietly picks up the salvageable fragments and goes back to work, undeterred. He is never content merely to bite off and colonize the small zones of consciousness that have come to signal contemporary poetry. Each line he writes reminds us that there is no cultural rainbow to catch us, no government program that will ensure that our half-assed musings are going to alter the conditions of the world we live in. All that satisfies him is work, because that is all that satisfies the Muse. And the end result may or may not be memorable or great. He is troubled by that, but he never stops to wiggle his ass at anyone because of it. Determining the value of a poet's work, he implies, is not the job of the poet.

For those who value poetry, meanwhile, it should be a comfort to know that a poet like Sibum is at work. When the completed book gets published – if it ever does – it will not be as slick as any of a half dozen volumes of verse that are published each year in this country. But in a different and older sense of poetry, it might turn out to be as large as Rilke's *Duino Elegies* or William Carlos Williams' *Desert Music* or Pindar's *Odes*. And that is the only measure of a poet's work that matters.

Books in Canada

CAREERS

During the late 1960s, between administration building occupations, anti-Vietnam War demonstrations, and occasional university classes, my first wife and I distracted ourselves with a board game called Careers. The game – no doubt updated and computerized by now – is still around. Back then it was a nice simple dice-and-icon movement game for ages eight years and up, meant to entertain adults and propagandize children – or maybe, as I'm discovering is the case with a lot of things, it is the other way round.

To begin the game, you're asked to choose a combination of love, fame and money. You then move around the game-board trying to acquire these by rolling the dice and making "career" choices. The first player to reach his or her quotas in all three categories wins.

What got me interested in Careers was that it appeared to contain a puzzling kind of Confucian logic, a variety that I, as a simple boy from northern British Columbia, couldn't quite fathom. For a few months we played the game incessantly, mostly at my insistence. I was at that point in my post-adolescence where I thought everything had a secure cause, and I'd arrogantly and erroneously begun to believe that the trick of succeeding at anything was a matter of figuring out what the biases in the rulebook were, and exploiting them. I got obsessed with determining exactly what the Careers formula for success was, and what logic lay behind it.

The formula should have been simple. The game provides only three criteria for success, and an equal division of one's quota of sixty points should have worked: twenty happiness, twenty fame, twenty money. But it didn't seem to. A slight over-balancing toward one goal invariably worked better – say, thirty happiness, twenty fame, and ten money. I deduced from this that the important biases in the game had been secretly hidden. Unfortunately, whenever I identified one and tried to exploit it, the bias displayed a certain instability that defied my attempts to fix and manipulate. It never occurred to me that the real bias might have been against stability itself, and I was too naive a logician – and inexperienced as an Orientalist – to realize that the companion to every rulebook is randomness. Like the rest of civilization I was overlooking an obscure item in The Western Rulebook – that games, business and life have different goals that alter the entire rulebook according to the situation one faces.

Occasionally our friends came over and played with us. One friend in particular came over a lot. Discretion keeps me from revealing his full name because he's still around, and would certainly find this episode in his life embarrassing. I'll call him J. He was two or three years older than we were, and a fairly respected poet. At the time, he'd just joined a Maoist splinter group which I won't name either because it's still around, and its members have a nasty habit of banging real or perceived critics over the head with lengths of Albanian-approved lumber or metal pipe.

J had his own reasons for playing Careers, and for a time he became at least as obsessed with the game as I was. As a Marxist-Leninist, however, his program was very different from mine. I was trying to pin down the precise parameters of what I thought was a rational logic system. He was demonstrating the virtue (if not the verity) of a philosophical principle. From his Marxist-Leninist point of view, love and fame were bourgeois distractions. He made money his sole choice – sixty money, zero fame, and piss on love.

I won a lot less frequently than I felt I should have, but J literally never won. Not that he cared about winning. Like all Marxist-Leninists he was more interested in demonstrating the gulf between the virtue of his principle and bourgeois reality and in denouncing the bourgeoisie for its lack of virtue. I could see exactly why he was losing, but my own lack of success was harder to figure. It seemed like whatever formula I happened to be following was temporarily the wrong one. I noted, with some annoyance, that whenever someone else chose a formula I'd just abandoned, it worked just fine.

What made me think about Careers again was that I ran into J recently in one of Vancouver's public libraries. He was wearing a beat-up trenchcoat and polyester pants and was carrying a shopping bag full of papers and books. I was looking a little more slick, but only slightly so – newer trenchcoat and a black leather shoulderbag full of books. I ran into him in the newspaper archive, where I was researching a series of irrational killings that occurred locally about eight years ago. I assumed he was there doing research too, probably on some aspect of the labour scene the Party had instructed him to infiltrate.

J is almost fifty years old now. His hair is iron grey and his body has thickened with middle age, his face is puffy from too many years of living on Kraft dinners and drinking cheap scotch late at night. If you saw him today you might mistake him for one of those Jehovah's Witnesses who stand on the streetcorner selling pamphlets and chewing the cud of utter certainty while they wait for Armageddon to begin. Or you might until his eyes betrayed him.

J's eyes are hungry and quick, and they speak of impulses he's never much wanted to confront or talk about. When he was younger the hunger had a distinct sexual character, and an astonishing number of women responded to it in kind. Now the hunger is more diffuse, less appetite and Eros than a chronic psychic malnutrition.

He told me he was writing a novel. Surprised, I asked him if he was writing it for the Movement. Years ago, the faction he joined had ordered him to stop writing anything more creative than cell reports and propaganda pamphlets. He'd complied without a protest.

He answered that he wasn't in the Movement anymore. "They, uh, the Movement and I parted company."

There was something about the way he said it that warned me that I shouldn't press him about it, but I did anyway. Hadn't he been with them for twenty years?

The precise figure turned out to be twenty-two years. Then, suddenly, the Movement had decided that they weren't "sure" of him anymore. Expelling him, he intimated darkly, was some sort of test.

When I asked him what it was a test of, he admitted ruefully that he didn't know, but said that it was in the nature of the Movement to be suspicious of its people.

To me that sounded cruel and stupid, and I said so, adding that as far as I could see, the most powerful element in every Marxist-Leninist organization was its internal police force. Then I asked him why people stayed inside such paranoid organizations for so long.

He deflected my question. "I'm not inside it now," he shrugged. "I'm out. That's why I'm trying to write a novel."

Here I hesitate. I must have done the same thing while I was talking to J, because I can't tell you the subject matter of his proposed novel. I didn't ask, or perhaps he told me and I didn't listen. Or maybe he didn't know what his novel was going to be about, and simply had the impulse and the ambition to write one because he'd once been a poet. Poets are, after all, the flaky cousins of novelists. For sure, the project of writing a novel bore an existential relationship to the rest of his career – which has been governed by a serial pursuit of large, noble, externalizing orderings of the universe.

I won't take odds on him completing the novel, and I'm even less optimistic that it will be readable if he does write it. I'm from the "use it or lose it" school, and for J it has probably been too damned long away. Besides that, I'm convinced that the same impulse that led him to join the Maoists and made him choose a sixty-point money formula in Careers will defeat him with a novel. The world has changed, even if Maoists and the novel haven't.

If I appear to be leading up to some strange remarks about the novel – as a literary and/or intellectual project – I am. Forty years ago, writing a novel was still a grand and noble project, one of the few refuges within which an individual could attempt to set everything relevant or true within a single frame and then to force those elements, by widely accepted authorial technologies and private courage, into a coherence – an order that explains everything outside it. Popular novels still do this today, from Stephen King to Harlequin romances, but now they have the subliminal intention of putting the reader into a moral and intellectual coma. Fantasy and entertainment have replaced enlightenment as the public purpose of most novels: quick, cheap holidays, as Stephen King has it.

I'm talking about a specific kind of novel in which the novelist sits hidden behind the sets and pulls the strings on his characters from above and beyond, telling us what they feel and think without ever testifying personally to the sources of data or the verities of his or her interpretation. It is a form that, interestingly, emerged clearly as the dominant literary form around the same time Marx and Engels were setting down the moral critique and empirical tenets of capitalist economics that Lenin and his friends later translated into crushing administrative apparatuses and police states.

Applied Marxism-Leninism has since been exposed as an inherently violent and brutalizing form of government that has very little scientific ground and no natural purchase in the human psyche, one that should be expunged from the human community as soon as possible. My "strange" proposition is that the puppeteer novel – a.k.a. the 19th century novel – similarly has been a disgraceful episode in the history of Western art, a drawn-out authoritarian incident which reasonably ought to be ending.

It seems to me that to be a responsible artist – at least since the Renaissance – has been to operate from contrary impulses to those that have powered the novel. Artists are supposed to render reality in all its complexities – without simplification, and without an ideological or formalist police force to keep the wild stuff out and the tame stuff either cowering in terror or asleep. Even the devotional art of the pre-Renaissance sought to express the beauty or justice of order, not its power or its capacity to isolate and manipulate.

The puppeteer novel has some curious and rarely examined origins. In its purest formulation, it was created for the rapidly growing European bourgeoisie of the 19th century, and was meant to be read aloud by the newly leisured heads of country mansions during the long and poorly illuminated evenings. The omniscient narrator allowed the reader to elude the testimonial format that characterized the narratives of the 18th century, reinforcing the reader/narrator's authority without making it conspicuous.

As readers and listeners became comfortable with the form, and as the circle of literate citizens began to spread beyond the upper middle classes, the procedure gathered a formal adjunct to it, one in which the novel has since invested its claim to verity. This adjunct is the "Fictional Agreement" in which the audience – or private readers, as it soon became – purposefully suspend disbelief in order to enter the fictional conceit without making potentially hostile comparisons.

The Fictional Agreement is an extremely sophisticated set of intellectual and cultural procedures, and it is unique to Western cultures. It is first of all provisional, and depends on the listener/reader suspending *and then reimposing* disbelief in an orderly sequence: intake first, comparative analysis second, synthesis third, and action last (and optional). In its purest instances, the Fictional Agreement has been a wonderful procedure. When a 19th century intellectual was confronted by an Emile Zola novel, for instance, all four steps were compulsory, and the expected effect was to create social and political change. In some instances, and to varying degrees, it succeeded.

Conditions have degenerated in a very odd way since the 19th century. Partly this is a result of the natural weakening of class and intellectual protocols as literacy spread to the point where it became merely a social or career asset rather than a prized social and political accomplishment – and a privilege. The disintegration of the Fictional Agreement accelerated in the aftermath of the Great War, which scrambled all of civilization's intellectual protocols by demonstrating that technological complexity was not married to social progress, and that it contains no inherently utopian program. Quite the opposite, the evidence showed. It continues to show this, now in much more vivid and hard-to-ignore ways.

It's no accident that the most important political result of the Great War – the Bolshevik revolution in Russia – instantly made a fundamental and cynical modification of the Marxist canon by placing an interpretive module between the masses and their revolutionary utopia. The revolutionary vanguard and its OGPU (or internal police) quickly sequestered and degraded each and every M-L revolution by interposing a new privileged class to govern in the interest of a stultifying and rapidly petrifying set of absolute values no group or individual could ever successfully embody. It also sacrificed natural justice, truth and humane compassion without a qualm to the dictates of dialectical materialism and its human vanguard.

The novel doesn't offer precise parallels, but the emergence of Lit Crit and *its* OGPU, the English Department, does have some remarkably similar characteristics. They have managed to extend the viability of the novel at least fifty years beyond its natural span – taking it and other forms to an advanced state of senility that undermines literate culture's capacity to meet the totalitarian challenge of consumerism and the Global Village.

The Leninist enterprise likewise probably wouldn't have survived the Second World War were it not for its immensely powerful internal police forces, which murdered millions and sent millions more to the Gulags in the decade after 1945. It helped give us, instead of a world community, a Cold War. The English Department gave us, instead of the triumph of liberal education, the decay of literature and a dictatorship of ego- and salary-driven genre specialists who have less intimate contact with the currents of culture and history than a tennis pro has. The result, as we begin the countdown to the millennium, is a world community with no sense of community, where the only shared goals are private – a trip to Disney World or to the local mall.

What does this have to do with Careers and with J's novel? Well, first of all, artists don't get to play at careers, and they aren't specialists or experts manipulating logic machines – LitCrit or Marxist-Leninism. Artists are supposed to be our generalists, our cultural synthesizers. When they stick themselves into careerist cannons and allow themselves (or their egos) to be shot out of them, they end up believing in tricks and in expertise, and wind up selling pamphlets on the street corner with all the other sociopathic entrepreneurs. If they're really talented, they might end up as a Stephen King – a rich prodigy and a kind of cultural idiot-savant with lots of sales impact and a huge audience, but no distinguishable cultural influence. Most often, they end up trying to count how many small-minded tenured faculty can be placed on the head of a diminishing budget, or, as in J's case, trying to convince people that Albania is the paradigm of the planet's political virtues.

This leads me to posit the existence of a mysterious substance that is never talked about, but which is a primary signal of artistic and intellectual failure. I call it impact dust. It is a fine metaphysical powder that obscures collective and individual vision, and breeds illusions of coherence and consistency that many people find comforting.

This was the secret of Stalin's power, Hitler's power, and it is the secret of television evangelists and others who make their living by exploiting moral and intellectual laziness, venality and gullibility. It also explains the durability and persistence of the novel, sort of. An artist who gives himself up to be shot out of a cannon – I can more or less specify "man" because women don't seem to be as drawn to this practice in any aspect of their physical, intellectual or emotional proclivities – creates impact dust in sufficient quantities to blind himself and very often those in the impact area. Impact dust so obscures the lineaments of practical *virtu* that it is easy to mistake the energy of the trajectory and impact for reality itself. When the source is a relatively ordinary person like J, only he and maybe a few others are going to be blinded. But we should remember that when the shell size is large, you get Nazi Germany, or Stalinist Russia, and people start dying.

Right now the air is so full of dust from minor impacts we seem to have lost track of the fact that the purpose of culture is not simply to produce aesthetic products for the English department to process. The purpose of culture is to create and invigilate our collective – as opposed to private – goals. We've also lost sight of the dense patterns of interactions by which the apparent randomness of experience and impulse cohere – not as belief or self-expression or absolute knowledge, but as nourishing texture and complexity. The randomness is part of the pattern, which is what both the novel and Marxism-Leninism tried to make disappear.

It *is* possible to recognize patterns of verity, and to trace the uncertain but substantial patterns of confluence into everyday life. To do so is the contract art seeks with everyday life. If we're to rediscover who or what or where we are, we'd better begin by recognizing that we can't determine it for ourselves alone anymore. Nor are we going to find it out within the comforts of ideology or senile formalisms. The absolute knowledge that is part and parcel of a conventional novel just isn't possible, and never was. Rulebooks, in art or in politics, should therefore be viewed with suspicion.

This is why I don't want to read J's novel – or, for that matter, any novel that doesn't mount a fundamental challenge to the way novels have been written and read for the last 150 years. I don't want such counterproductive artifacts to be taken as a geniune response to life in the 1990s. Careers? Well, that's just a silly game.

Quarry

POSTMODERN FUSIONS, CONFUSIONS, AND HYPERMODERNISM

At the heart of the postmodernist elan in contemporary literature are two connected phenomena: 1) litcrary genres that are showing signs of extreme confusion as to their verity and value, and 2) a distinct movement toward the creation of new genres at least partly through the fusion of relevant elements in the old ones. For me, the issues inherent in those phenomena are not playful ones, and the questions raised by the issues certainly are not rhetorical.

Whether or not the confusions and fusions of the postmodernist enterprise will be adequate to protect our heritage as *Homo sapiens* against the culturally destructive forces of consumerist globalism is the most important question faced by literature today, and by literate culture itself. If it is not answered soon, I fear there will be no literature in the future except perhaps as a minor heritage activity, or as a raw material for industrial academia. The latter already overshadows literature in the number of practitioners and in public funding it receives. Literate culture and its imaginative practitioners could soon cease to have any role – curatorial or otherwise – to play in either the energizing, regulating or humanizing of civil societies.

For as long as I can recall, I have held the conviction that artists have profound civil responsibilities. It may be because when I was a child my mother read long tracts of Shelley's verse to me, or perhaps because I grew up in a small town in the chilly northern wilderness of British Columbia where everyone had civil responsibilities. Whatever the source, my work has been energized by a sense of responsibility and civil curiosity rather than political or ideological ambition. I have deliberately lived and worked close to the sources of political power, but I have been privileged enough to exercise a curiosity about why power exists and how it is distributed without having to be terrorized by questions of who is in power, and of how to either please or avoid them. It's a privilege I accept without gratitude because it contains ironies and indignities that I am daily made to suffer through.

In my view, the writer's social responsibility is to understand and interpret the nature of civil culture for his or her fellow citizens, and to expose the discrepancies between program reality and actuality – whether or not anyone wants them interpreted or exposed. In our epoch, this responsibility involves addressing the conditions under which fundamental human values are exercised – values like kindness, the right to laugh, and to take pleasure in the particularities of people, things and processes, along with a host of other "simple" behaviours that appear to be disappearing as the fundamentalisms of economic globalism sweep the planet.

In addition, the writer's responsibility – and this is a social and a professional responsibility – is to tell the tale of the tribe in ways that bring its associational truths and inherited intellectual technologies to as many people as possible – without sacrificing its complexity to propaganda or to exclusionary languages or dialects. This is, I believe, the true meaning and purpose of what Dante called the vernacular. It is something that can only exist in a democracy.

The etymological root of the word "narrative" is the Greek word *gnarre*: to know. Since Homer, narrative technologies have been a response both to the means available for gathering and disseminating knowledge, and to the kinds of things people need to know. The Iliad and Odyssey, as Eric Havelock revealed some years ago, were devised – or evolved – as encyclopedias and cultural operations manuals rather than works of art. Their mnemonic hexameters and other devices gave specific instructions about how to launch ships and make sacrifices to the gods while they transferred their historical summary of Mycenaean Greece to its Dorian conquerors. Both texts were meant to be used, and like all great art they were meant to subvert and civilize by engendering a taste for complexity. I do not think they were meant to be admired for their aesthetic subtleties.

Until recently narrative forms have largely been a response to strategic and utilitarian necessities rather than aesthetic demands. The complicated symbolic encodings of the Medieval troubadours were primarily a response to authoritarian repression – if you said what was really on your mind, someone might chop your head off. Likewise, the narrative strategies of the novel, particularly after the 18th century, were at least partly a means to elude censorship and authoritarian violence. The omniscient narrator of the 19th century European novel also has another, slightly different, but no less pragmatic origin – in the uneven rise of literacy there, where reading aloud was a prestigious and primary social activity, it was a method of asserting pedagogic and familial authority. Likewise, I'm aware that in some countries – the Third World, mostly, now that the Soviet Bloc has disintegrated – the strategies of indirection and symbolic encoding remain relevant.

None of the above conditions of knowledge or authority any longer pertain to the society I come from, which is a minor First World English-speaking democracy. Since the Second World War censorship and other forms of direct informational suppression have more or less vanished, and illiteracy, at least if you accept the official explanation, has become more a cognitive disability than an economic or political one.

At the root of these changes is the massive growth in the efficiency and universality of communication technologies, which have made direct censorship virtually impossible to administer. At first this "globalization" seemed to promise an educational and informational Golden Age. What has evolved instead is the Global Village, which employs data atomization, overload, trivialization and mass con-duitization to create a monoculture that deprives citizens of specific and useable knowledge as effectively as any directly repressive society that has ever existed. English-speaking North Americans and most Western Europeans (I wouldn't presume to speak for other countries) are not afraid to understand or criticize our political, social and intellectual culture. The problem most of us have is that we can't recognize any specific culture among the Disney icons, the televised incitements to violence and conspicuous consumption, and the consumer franchises that bleed local economies and cultures of their vitality. Most of us have also been divested of the tools needed to analyze and evaluate where we are and what is happening to us.

Meanwhile, the novel, in particular, has lost its cultural authority even though it remains the flagship of conventional literature. In part this is because one cannot get an angle on the daily news from it, which is what most people want now, but the truer cause is that the novel offers no formal insights about how to sort the overabundance of data coming at us. It says nothing about how or why, in the midst of such technological and informational wealth, the communications system we live enmeshed in seeks mainly to deceive and manipulate us.

With its characteristically omniscient narrator, the mainstream novel participates in the Christian delusion (now really a neo-Darwinian determinism) that the world, in its chaos of forms and appearances, is ultimately subject to order – be it divine, paradigmatic or holographic. The new critical mind that is emerging from the informationalization of the planet, by contrast, demands a much more heterogeneous structuring of reality. The cognitive and conceptual toolbox needed to apprehend reality is very much larger and more diverse than the one that novelists have settled around.

Marshall McLuhan, who first recognized, in the 1950s, the tend-

ency of information-driven societies toward a simultaneous atomization of perception and an implosion of intellectual disciplines, said
we would need elevated pattern discernment, improved pixel matrix
scanning strategies, and the capacity to leap from discipline to technical dialect to wide-open phenomenology without irritability or
loss of attention. He recognized that the human species is undergoing
a retooling of thought processes more profound than anything that
has occurred since our ancestors stumbled out of the caves and began
to live in agricultural communities seven to ten thousand years ago.

McLuhan believed that to survive the destructive effects of the
changes, human beings must become weavers of information, and
masters of its mass conduits – or be devoured by the productive force
of the systems. Whether or not the changes occurring – or not occurring – in literary narrative techniques are a significant part of that
general retooling of the human mind is not clear. It seems to me that
the changes in our literary forms are lagging far behind.

In 1986, I published a book titled *Cambodia: A Book For People
Who Find Television Too Slow*. What I meant by the rather strange
title was that I wanted to produce a text that was "faster" informa-
tionally than contemporary communication technology. But at the
same time as I moved to make my text formally much more open and
transparent than most literary texts, I wanted to retain and transform
the textual density which literature has traditionally sought.

To achieve my goals, I made two thoroughly existential organizational decisions. One was to engage the most difficult subject matter
I could locate. The second was to let the content of the book dictate
the form it would take – to let it be, in the jargon of computers, con-
tent-driven. The result was a book with a primary text consisting of
thirteen "episodes", and a 25,000-word subtext that runs across the
bottom third of the page as what one critic called a "marauding foot-
note".

The "difficult subject matter" I settled on, as the book's title indicates, was Cambodia. As a Canadian in 1984, I understood almost
nothing about Cambodia, having concerned myself to that point, as
most First World writers do, with narratives about the private,

twisted epiphanies allowed us in a privatized, twisted world. I wrote stories with beginnings, middles and ends, dialogue ratios, and the rest of the obsolete paraphernalia of the Fictional Agreement.

I set out to research what has taken place over the last several decades in Indochina, and began, in the absence of a blueprint or map, to write what appeared to be a long essay on my chosen subject. But when I began to gather the magnitude of what happened to the Cambodian people, first through the 1969 U.S. invasion and subsequent bombing, and then with the Khmer Rouge holocaust of 1975-79, I realized that what I was looking at was an attempt to suppress and erase the individual memories and imaginations of seven million people who had been deemed expendable – then and still – by virtually the entire world community.

I also began to note, uneasily, that there are uncomfortable parallels to this extermination of memory and imagination within the media-saturated world I live in. I began to track those parallels, and let them connect wherever they had a will to. Eventually, the record of the parallels formed the book's primary text, with the essay on Cambodia acting as its subtext – just as the events in Cambodia, it seems to me, constitute the chilling subtext to my own world. A 1990 book, *Public Eye: An Investigation into the Disappearance of the World*, employs essentially the same method and format, but with the subject matter of the disappearance of particularity and local culture.

The texts of both books have a strange appearance, but that isn't why I'm bringing them up. Whatever conventional literary merit they have (which is not much, at times) they are attempts to respond to the reality of changed informational identities and densities, and to the indisputable fact that individual human receptors are being shaped, manipulated and frequently disabled by our mass communications systems. The books are also attempts to respond to the fact that the arts in general, and literature in particular, have ceased to be in the vanguard of cultural suasion or production.

I've taken some of my cues from writers like Manuel Puig, John Berger, and Eduardo Galeano, all of whom have been willing to crash or mix genres and disciplines in order to renew the discourse that must be at the root of artistic enterprise. The other cues, it seems to me, are in the information systems we deal with daily.

From Berger, a writer who writes, as I do, slowly and with difficulty, I learned that style is merely a clarity of thought and density of sources. Neither of my two recent books could have been written without word processors, which make it infinitely easier to track multiple subjects and themes, and to contextualize them. Using them also makes it difficult to fetishize the act of composition. I used word processing to overcome my biggest shortcoming – my own stupidity and laziness – developing a method of composition that involves repeated revision, which for me involves rethinking as much as re-writing. Most of what I publish (in book form, at least) has been revised, word by word and concept by concept, at least thirty or forty times. Properly used, word processors can be a wonderful aid to intellectual courage. They also do away with the need for secretarial courage, of which I have very little.

The thirteen years I spent working as an urban planner gave me a familiarity with data manipulation and integration as a conceptual tool. Planning also taught me that civil coherence is a basic human social need and a primary instinct, but that both the need and the instinct have been massively subverted by a plethora of uncontrolled and expanding binary systems that have logic-driven rather than humane determinations.

Urban planning also gave me a working understanding of modernism and postmodernism as active technical ideologies and as architectural physicalities. The way that built forms impinge on human space and reveal the demonic biases in the cognitive structures through which we experience, interpret or avoid the world around us has been a revelation. It has also skewed – or perhaps corrected – my view of literature.

Modernism, which is characterized by a belief in the powers of expert knowledge and centralized functionalism, does not work because it chronically overlooks the fragile complexities – organic and intellectual – of the human species. In a sense, it has populated the world with one-dimensional, soulless efficiencies and competing monocultures, just as architectural modernism has filled our cities with soullessly "efficient" skyscrapers.

Postmodernism, which seems to correct those tendencies, fails because it never challenges the basic premises of modernism. It has become a tyranny of professionals and experts, who undertake to make all history and culture simultaneous and relative, but are unconscious agents of a cybernetic monoculture in which the feedback circuits are atrophied by secret syntaxes and intellectual black boxes that protect professional privileges but render them servile or irrelevant. Postmodernist architecture, particularly in its commercial form, best reveals the weaknesses of postmodernism. It is modernism with bric-a-brac and high colour, and its ultimate expression – the consumer megamall – is really a skyscraper laid on its side. It has a few more entrances and exits, but the questions of whether we should enter or leave, or why, as human beings, we should want to use them or express ourselves within and through them, are broached no more frequently.

Very tentatively, our best architects are now re-examining the premises of modernist functionalism and postmodernism's relativist Latin in the light of current knowledge of the complex texturing of the human organism and its associative infrastructure and interdependencies. What we're now beginning to see is a "hypermodernism" that accounts for what we know about ourselves and our planet, recognizes the inherent violence of monocultural systems, and addresses the fundamental questions of civil existence: why are we alive, and how should we continue? These are the questions at the root of all art, and as in every age, the vernacular must be reinvented in order to ask them.

A hypermodernist literature to parallel it is clearly needed. A con-(fusion) of narrative forms is, hopefully, the signal that such a literature is dawning.

Capilano Review

SOMETHING IS WRONG WITH ALICE MUNRO

You can relax. Canada's most respected writer is doing fine. She's probably living in one of those small, exquisite Ontario towns, writing small, exquisite stories. As far as I know she's in good spirits and her health is sound. Phones Audrey Thomas, Robert Weaver and John Metcalf on successive nights to chat, I hear.

Maybe I should qualify what I just said. I'm one of her readers, not a personal friend. I'm certainly not an enemy. I've never actually met her, but from what I'm told I'm confident that I'd like and admire her, just like I do her stories.

But while I'm cheerfully prepared to go on liking her stories, the fact that she's become an almost unassailable cultural icon has begun to trouble me. As Canada threatens to break apart, and as fewer and fewer people regard literature as an integral part of their daily cultural apparatus, I'm developing the nagging instinct that I shouldn't like Alice Munro stories as much as I do.

Why? Quite simply, her stories are too *small* to be thought of – as they are almost unanimously by those with a grasp of Canadian writ-

ing that extends beyond Farley Mowat – as the best and most important literary artifacts Canada produces. For sure, Alice Munro stories
are almost perfectly structured and crafted. Yes, they're filled with
miracles of subtlety so intense that they drive educated folks over the
age of 40 nearly out of their comas. CanLit industrialists across the
nation shudder with delight when a new volume of her work hits the
bookstores, knowing that if a free desk copy doesn't come their way
unasked, in two or three years they will find it important enough that
they'll saunter down to a bookstore and actually buy a copy.

You may have already noted, reader, that my complaint is not
really about Alice Munro the person or writer, but about the conditions of literary culture that can make a talented but somewhat antiquarian miniaturist our most revered living writer. As a master of the
modernist short story, Munro's skills and formal preoccupations are
those of a 19th century writer. At best, she has mastered a literary
form that stopped bending people's minds a half century ago.

I know what I'm suggesting is horribly impolite, but don't dismiss
me yet. Have a hard look at the conditions of political, technological
and cultural life under which we now labour. Then have a look at
what the modernist short story sets out to accomplish.

A formally correct short story develops a small texture of reality –
usually centering on one or two characters – and turns it in subtle
moral and material lighting conditions so that we see how wonder-
fully complex and fragile human beings are, and how textured psychological reality is. Somewhat shyly and indirectly, such stories are
a defence of what is humane and good. They are also, provided that
one is trained to such things, aesthetically gratifying and even interesting. But the modernist short story is still a very small bite at the
enormously enlarged complexity of the human condition. The short
story, notwithstanding Freud and Jung, and with a cold stare at 75
years of essentially unproductive psychoanalytic attempts to tamper
with the human psyche without tampering with the violent world it
operates in, is diminishing in its relevance and centrality to the
human condition.

Let me put this as crassly as I can. What good is the modernist short story in a world where Walt Disney's heirs and shareholders are running our national and global culture, where mainstream North American consciousness has been overrun with consumerism and cartoons? What real defence of what is humane and good does it offer against the grinning professionals of the Cosby Universe?

If I were prepared to be completely bloody-minded, I'd point out that most of the characters Alice Munro offers us are mainly wounded people slipping inexorably into incapacity. Most of the subtleties she renders are diminishments, retreats into privileged silence, anguish or sentimentality. Again and again, her protagonists can imagine no other material world than the one they're in. But I respect Munro's skills, and I enjoy subtleties, so I won't point out any of those things.

Instead, let me make a proposition. It is that every era has its central subject matter, one that provides essential focus to artistic and political life. These subject matters constitute something like what Mayakovsky called the "social command". What I'm talking about is half way between that and a moral imperative. In the 1950s and 1960s, when the ascendant literary figures of our own time were in their formative stages, particularly in North America, that subject matter was centred around liberation – sexual liberation, the economic liberation of the working class, women's liberation from the cultural domination of males. In its most simple formulation, it was about the individual, and how individuals got what they wanted and needed. If the era were to be reduced to a single question it would be this: *Why can't (or how do) I get what I want out of life?*

Such concerns bred the artistic milieu of Alice Munro in Canada, and writers like Toni Morrison, John Updike or Raymond Carver in the United States. Each is a master of the modernist short story, the perfect vehicle for dramatizing the subtle permutations of an era preoccupied with private liberations. (This same milieu also created Norman Mailer and the Harlequin universe, but that's an issue I'll have to defer.)

Meanwhile, it seems to me that in the 1980s and the 1990s, the central questions and focusing subject matter have changed – quite dramatically. Today we're less citizens than we are consumers, and in our willy-nilly rush to get what we want, we've discovered that private liberation doesn't create a liberated world. In burning up the planet's resources, we've driven ourselves to the point of intellectual, economic, and ecological collapse. This era's subject matter seems to be focused on issues of government and governance – of resources, information, and ourselves. And today's question – not yet entirely clear – might be this one: *Why (or how) in an era of total information, is everyone and everything deceiving us?*

I don't think the modernist short story gives us adequate equipment to approach that question. It's a different game now, and the rules and tools are going to be different – perhaps radically different.

Incidentally, I am thoroughly aware that the demand for moral competence from literature puts me on unfashionable and even dangerous ground – on intellectual quicksand, actually. But if I take the moderately unorthodox step of recognizing that culturally significant narrative is not eternally boundaried by the regulations concerning 19th century "fictional" narrative, the quicksand turns out to be merely a shallow pothole. If I take yet another step, this time to examine the degree to which modern media, particularly television, have corrupted and co-opted fictional narrative as they have literally everything else, the perspective changes altogether. Suddenly, the relativism of contemporary literary practice starts to look like either another shuck for maintaining an unexamined status quo, or an unforgiveable kind of naivety.

Just so the record is straight, I'd dearly love to live in a world in which the perceptual universe of someone like Alice Munro had real cultural and, better still, political currency. Like most writers, I'm more comfortable working with the problems of private consciousness. After all, that's what I was trained to do. I'm also a former Ezra Pound scholar, and I have the deepest possible respect for the literary traditions of Western civilization. A part of my nature would love to believe, as Pound did, that if we all read the Great Books and honoured the Great Writers, local and global, all the evils in the world would disappear. For sure, Brian Mulroney would not be Canada's prime minister, Dan Quayle would be delivering letters for the post office in some midwest American town, women would be treated equitably, Pol Pot would be dead, and so forth. But I'm not so blinded by mortgages and personal fitness classes and croissants that I miss seeing that we live in a world that is emphatically *not* respectful of Alice Munro's perceptual universe. Instead, what I see is a world that is daily becoming even less respectful of it, one that is declining into a new kind of ignorance and barbarity.

Sales of literary fiction have been diminishing for almost a decade. In Canada, the average sales of a literary fiction title is now well below 2000 copies, and that's factoring in Alice Munro, Margaret Atwood, Professor Davies and W.P. Kinsella – not very good compared to the 20,000 to 30,000 a run-of-the mill Harlequin romance does, and positively anemic compared to the millions who watch Cosby each week on the idiot box.

The problem doesn't lie entirely with the audience, or with the power of consumerist-oriented media. Increasingly, I'm convinced that the reluctance of writers to examine the formal properties and boundaries of literature has left written literature less able to capture today's realities than other artistic (and commercial) media.

So, instead of whining about it or predicting a cultural Apocalypse, let me propose a few changes that might begin to rectify the situation. The changes I'd propose follow pretty much what has gone on in nearly every other artistic discipline. But their application to literature, because the medium of literature is language, and because literature has a historical kinship with discourse, might have considerably more dramatic results than it has had in other disciplines. By making a radical adoption of the assemblage techniques used in other art forms, literature could make a belated but profound re-entry into mainstream 20th century culture and thought.

Explaining what that might involve requires an examination of today's key question noted above. The question asks us, first of all, to reverse most of the perceptual priorities that have served literature during our lifetime. If we try to answer it, the structure and content of what is coming at us becomes more important than what kinds of needs and abilities we give expression to. The integrity of our receiving apparatus and the sincerity of our interpretation will become far less meaningful. What will count are the number and complexity of field receptors that can be brought into play, and the sophistication of data interpretation.

At the very least, the situation calls for writers to have a long, cold look at the sanctity of literary genres, and their separation from discourse, particularly in fiction and poetry. Historiography, reportage, philosophical analysis and a massive influx of data also need to be brought into the legitimate – and even obligatory – working apparatuses of literary writers, along with a dose of murderous scepticism concerning the word "fiction".

A first step for writers to make would be to examine the field to determine which of our literary forms don't adequately address the question or are obsolete. An obvious method of doing that would be to see which have been superceded by other narrative mediums like television and film. Here, it quickly becomes apparent that if the sole criterion to determine "effectiveness" was audience appeal, we'd have to abandon literary fiction altogether to those media, except for the narrow market aimed at those who use fiction to render themselves semi-conscious during periods of voluntary or involuntary inactivity – hospital stays, train or plane trips, bad marriages, etc. That isn't good enough, just as determining the value of a literary work in terms of its internal aesthetic consistencies isn't good enough, although exactly what criteria writers should be using is far from apparent.

Probably the best way to proceed is to determine the contexts in which printed literature remains more effective and efficient than any other medium. For instance, what film and television do not do well at all is to transfer the complexity and verticality of reality – the parataxis of private, political and universal instrumentation that penetrates events. With rare exceptions, both mediums tend to sacrifice parataxis to sleekness and tones. Likewise, neither medium naturally supports feedback, contingency, or leisurely review. A literature of assemblage would turn itself to those gaps and confidently develop them. Yet in fact, the formal timidity of literature over the last four decades has done almost the opposite. During the 20th century the re-academization of knowledge has effectively given over the universal to science and philosophy, the political to journalism and the social sciences, leaving literature to dither politely over those rapidly shrinking precincts we hope are private.

Literature originally meant "written thought", and it's written thought that needs to be renovated if literature is to continue to have even the slightest cultural value in the future. Writers need to invade every other intellectual discipline, not as dedicated specialists but as intellectual generalists – as conceptual assemblers seeking to secure the full vertical density of human reality.

Right now, the field is relatively empty and open. In recent years, John Berger, Primo Levi, Eduardo Galeano and a few others have all made profound forays into it. Because women writers have had less reason to support the status quo, they've more generally been trying to make inroads from several directions and under ideologically difficult and variable dispensations. And of course, Marshall McLuhan overflew the field 25 years ago, but he was flying so high he mistook it for the Global Village and thought it would belong to television – or God. It doesn't, and it can't.

But Alice Munro, and the majority of fiction writers today, don't even know the field exists. And that is what is wrong with Alice Munro.

Capilano Review / Vancouver Review

MARGARET ATWOOD'S ACHIEVEMENT

Most writers become interesting, I think, when they recognize that it is not themselves and their inner life but the world and the things that go on in it that are worth writing about. Generally, it's a signal that the preliminaries are over, and that maturity (a rare occurrence in this culture) has arrived. That hasn't quite been the case with Margaret Atwood. She's always been interesting, even in her worst moments. But her 1991 volume of short stories, *Wilderness Tips*, is a signal, if anyone needed it, that she is now a mature writer in possession of a truly remarkable array of powers.

I used to dislike Margaret Atwood. Partly the dislike was the product of simple envy, but part of it she earned. It wasn't just that she subjected me to a vicious verbal beating around 1970 when I tried to skewer her at a party with a clumsy insult that I, in my innocence, mistook for a witty barb. For many years, Atwood acted as a hit-person for the Canadian Family Compact, and she wrote some questionable books. *Survival* was a Northrop Frye-induced piece of mechanized intellectual careerism designed (knowingly or not) to put her on the forefront of CanLit theory. The premise of *Survival* was sophomoric, and it helped to produce a sophomoric view of Canadian literature with which our universities are still deluding young students. More damning, from an artistic point of view, was that in her early work (*Surfacing* instantly comes to mind) the characters modeled after Atwood were always more interesting and smarter than anyone else. Generally they got all the best insights and speeches, and the joke was invariably – and usually painfully – at someone else's expense.

Such excesses are understandable, in retrospect. She was, after all, working a field blessed with an overabundance of upper middle class males, most of them pretenders and jerks who thought women were either sports or walking kitchen utensils. Back then Atwood was very ambitious, and she was tough and bloody-minded. It was her gift (and sometimes her curse) to have no tolerance for fools or foolishness – something that a lot of Canadian literati learned to respect the hard way. I did. For a while I amused myself by pointing out her resemblance to Miss Piggy from the Muppets, and waited for the time when I could safely take revenge. Circumspect chap that I am, I assumed from the beginning that safe revenge would probably have to involve an armed satellite circling the planet, and I didn't hold my breath while I waited.

Others, I've recently noted, haven't been quite so circumspect. Last year, for instance, multiculture booster, French-Canadian penis and Canadian colonial furniture aficionado Scott Symons launched an attack on Atwood in the *Idler* that was distinguished by its rancour, bad prose, and poor aim. I reread his article recently, to see if I could figure out what was behind it. At first I merely rediscovered what a lousy writer Symons is. At one point, for instance, he describes Atwood's importance with the following deathless sentences (and sentence fragments): ". . . she managed to embody both the surge of feminism and the development of the national identity. With Ms. Atwood the two items appeared as one. Perhaps because the advance of the Canadian identity seemed to go hand in hand with the detumescence of the Canadian male."

It would be fun to speculate about what Symons thinks the "surge of feminism" the "development of the national identity" or the "detumescence of the Canadian male" are, why he keeps putting verbs associated with sexuality where ordinary nouns ought to be, or why, later on in the article, he would be dumb enough to quote Norman Mailer as an expert on female behaviour. But enough is enough. I think I know what was behind the attack. Symons, and a lot of others, simply can't stand the fact that Atwood is unapologetically – and successfully – who she is and what she knows. They can't stand the fact that she writes the best sentences currently being written in this country – and that she is a world-class writer who remains world-class no matter what she thinks, speaks or writes about. A long time ago, her intolerance of fools may have been seeded by a fear of appearing to be one herself. In 1991, she seems uniquely incapable of intellectual or artistic foolishness.

What I'm saying here is that it is time for us to assess Margaret Atwood's skills as a mature writer and not as a shit-kicking national *enfant terrible*. She's grown, and what one encounters in *Wilderness Tips* is a different writer than the one we read even a decade ago. She still has the hard-edged persona and confidence, and a similar but enhanced technical and intellectual virtuosity. But she's more generous now, less bitchy, and her focus has a truly marvellous depth and patience.

The majority of the stories in *Wilderness Tips* are about women navigating their way through the wilderness of contemporary life. The landscapes are a long way from the English Department wilderness of *Survival*, where every viewpoint is buffered by institutional ideology or partisan fashion, and the wilderness is about as threatening as a parking lot full of Winnebagos. The wilderness of *Wilderness Tips* is the one we all live in – whether we admit it or not – where the sexual and political have become thoroughly confused, and there is no idyllic ideological campground at the end of the trail – and certainly no serviced parking bays for academic Winnebagos.

Unlike the old Atwood heroines, the women in these stories are multidimensional, filled with half-realized strengths and half-recognized vulnerabilities. They get victimized, but they are seldom merely helpless victims, and the victimizations are never abstract. When they hurt, you see why. When they grow, you believe it because the circumstances of the story justify or command it. There is not a single moment of rhetorical spiritualization in these stories, which in the current partisan environment we have to think and write and read in, is a kind of miracle.

The males in the stories are treated with the same sure hand, and they are accorded a similar dignity – that of being vulnerable inhabitants of a wilderness. One of the most moving stories in the volume, "Isis In Darkness", records the attempt of a male narrator to come to terms with the life and death of a wraith-like woman whose life, he senses, is contrary and interlinear to his own. Atwood is able to reverse the shop-worn Osiris/Isis contrarium without falsifying the particularities or the sensitivities of either protagonist. Even the much-ballyhooed alleged portrait of Robert Fulford in the story titled "Uncles" is a characterization rather than a caricature. Given Fulford's dumb public response to it, the characterization seems extremely generous. Fulford *does* look like Mr. Weatherbee, and he *does* talk and write like he's got a fruit flan stuck in his throat.

The first time I read the story it didn't occur to me that Atwood might be taking revenge on someone, and if it had, I wouldn't have thought it was either significant or cruel. Everyone who has a brain larger than a walnut knows that good writers always draw their characters at least partly from real life. And anyway, the story is more a portrait of a now-common type of female media figure – someone like, say, Barbara Frum or Leila Paul. I thought Atwood was drawing a sharper edge along that figure than on the rather pathetic male Fulford has decided is an insult to his august person. One could equally take offense at the fact that Atwood drew on Gwen McEwen for the character of Selena in "Isis in Darkness" – at least until one woke up and began to pay attention to what these stories are really about, and how swiftly and surely they move.

I guess what I'm saying here is that I trust the stories, and that I

have come to trust Atwood. She does not belittle, she does not fal-
sify, and she does not trivialize anyone or anything. I happened to be
at my family's annual reunion in the B.C. interior while I was reading *Wilderness Tips*. As the weekend wore on, and as I read and reread the stories, I began to see the people around me – not quite
through Atwood's eyes – but with the kind of empathetic attention to
emotional nuance and detail the fictions of *Wilderness Tips* invoke. I
began to see the members of my own family more fully and generously, and I discovered that a few of them were more complex and
dignified than I'd been able to recognize. I was grateful for the experience.

That's the secret of Atwood's mature vision: that Canadians – or
most Canadians – live in an armed and subtly violent world in which
the conflicts are mostly covert or unrecognized, and that most of
them are cruel and stupid and sectarian. But no one, in her vision,
needs to (or should) be completely helpless or unarmed. As the circumstance arises, we can use our broadaxes and compasses to defend
or relocate ourselves. Hence the book's title is an accurate one.
These really are *Wilderness Tips*, and they are sensible and timely
ones, the best that anyone I've read has offered up in a long time.

I trust her skills and her motives because she's earned the trust,
just as I've come to trust and follow her lead in the arena of cultural
and sexual politics. Rather than pick her apart or view her achievements with envy, we ought to be trying to talk her into running for
prime minister – provided it allowed her enough time to go on writing. And obviously, I've cancelled my plan for a satellite attack.

Books in Canada

BRINGING BACK
PHILIP K. DICK

It's hard to get the superlatives about Philip K. Dick in order. IIe is among the most original writers science fiction has produced. Along with Ursula Le Guin, he wrote the most interesting sentences that have graced the genre. He was, again with Ursula Le Guin, among its most sophisticated social thinkers, and among its better science interpreters. What he gave his readers, better than any writer since Franz Kafka, was the sensation of what it is like to live in a world where all appearances deceive, a world in which the commonplace has lost its familiarity and safety. For Kafka the lurking threat that undermined reality was mechanization and bureaucracy. For Dick the threats were nuclear holocaust and the Mall, and he could – and still can – make you taste their terrors.

Personally, he was a domestic flake and a paranoid fruitcake who lived on the edge of addictive psychosis and collapse. His life history isn't a pleasant one, but like everything else about Dick, it is informative. Like no other writer I know of, his transformation of the details of his private life into fiction is almost completely transparent. It reveals the extraordinary courage of a man for whom mass extinction was a daily threat he was able to ward off only by writing stories about it.

Dick was born in Chicago, moved to California when he was two years old, and lived almost his entire life there. He died in 1982 at the age of 53. He spent most of his adult life in Berkeley, travelling rarely and usually with great discomfort brought on by a number of psychosomatic afflictions. He married (and divorced) five times, had two daughters, did not live house beautiful or happily, and was, by different accounts, charming and brilliant, egocentric, generous, erratic, crazy. Some of his wackiness and irascibility, at least until 1974, was the result of his over-use of various drugs, particularly speed. But he wrote more than 40 novels and 200 stories and kept up a massive correspondence, along with a 10,000-page unpublished diary.

Most non-aficionados of sci-fi, if they recognize Dick's name at all, know him as the author of the stories on which the 1982 movie classic *Blade Runner*, and the more recent *Total Recall*, were based. That's their misfortune. For those who have read his books and don't have their eyes blinkered by the English department's antiquarian fetishization of literary forms, it's an odds-on bet that if books are still being read a century from now – if stories are being told and listened to at all – two or three of Philip K. Dick's novels are likely to be among the books to which people will look to understand this era, with its obsessions about subliminal manipulation of consciousness and its trauma-wracked fascination with the general origins and limits of consciousness.

What is it about Philip K. Dick's stories that is so compelling? Maybe it's that even at their mechanical worst, they're rooted squarely in our sacred ground. They're operas about ideas, and Dick's fictional portrayal of these ideas is skilled enough that if he'd been a 19th century Russian operating in the Christian/socialist philosophical matrix, his name might have been Dostoyevsky. Dick happened to be a late 20th century American operating in the science/capitalism arena, where production-oriented paradigms are preferred to ideas, and where fiction, as it becomes our universal social condition, is instinctively distrusted the moment it demands anything more than a mental holiday. Dick is therefore passed over – by North Americans more than by Europeans, who seem to have an inkling of his importance – merely as a gifted but loony pulp writer. What makes him doubly difficult for North Americans to accurately value is that he's much more than a symbolic and static cipher whirling in the cross-currents and eddies of fashionable thinking. Dick was actively tooling sophisticated ideas, dramatizing them wildly in his novels, and being privately obsessed and victimized by his own insights. He's us, but at blender velocities.

For those just beginning to discover Philip K. Dick there's a recently published biography that can help. It's called *Divine Invasions: A Life of Philip K. Dick*, by Lawrence Sutin. Like most of Dick's stories, Sutin's biography is filled with sobering revelations about life, and as biographies go, it's a fairly unusual one.

Ours is a culture that avidly consumes biographies of people who have lived their lives with all the second thoughts of a kamikaze pilot. Because that's the way we're taught to live our lives, we're all ears and eyes for the hyperdrive dithering of a Zsa Zsa Gabor or a Donald Trump, but we have difficulty focusing on the life of a man like Philip K. Dick, whose day-to-day existence literally frothed with the troubled subtexts of our time.

The way Dick lived and wrote doesn't make a biographer's work easy, either. The trouble begins with the most simple problems – such as his name. One hesitates instinctively to call Philip K. Dick by his last name. It sounds like a first name, and it contains a built-in insult. If not that, his full name, Philip K. Dick, is a tongue-twister – pronounce it five times quickly and you've got a sore tongue and the giggles. Compounding this petty but quite real difficulty is Dick's peculiar approachableness – in his fiction, and, apparently, in his life. He invites us to think of him most easily as "Phil". Sutin calls him that throughout the biography, and it occasionally causes him, and the reader, to lose perspective.

But then what *do* you call a man who, like Dick, habitually invites you inside his brain, then suffers from bouts of acute paranoia concerning strangers and secret government organizations dedicated to manipulating or crushing individual imagination and will? How much different would Dick's career have been had he been born with a name like Thorstein Veblen or Gore Vidal?

Much more profound difficulties than his name abound. Dick isn't a conventional biographical subject because his life and work cross boundaries, and because both so chronically mix the sublime with the silly that it's often very hard to keep a straight face.

In addition, the writing and the ideation in his novels is woefully uneven. Privately, he led the kind of chaotic, demonic lifestyle that has caused the following generations of Americans to run directly into the clutches of leaders like Ronald Reagan (himself a man so inner-directed that he will probably read his deathbed words from cue-cards). Dick's personal struggle with inner chaos makes the ideation of his books uneven. When he's trivial he's really trivial. Other times, he is so close to both incoherence and inspired insight that it is nerve-wracking. But he can take you so close to the Heart of Darkness that reading him is frequently a psychically messy experience. For all that it's science fiction, one can sometimes feel the excoriations of Dick's mind and body as he struggles to articulate. You never quite know where you are when you're reading Dick, or how important what he's chasing truly is.

Another problem – like the others, a mixed blessing – is that Dick was astonishingly prolific, despite the domestic mayhem he surrounded himself with. Finally (for this incomplete list of complications, at least) in 1974 he had a series of (how shall I put this neutrally?) . . . ah, *extra-normal experiences* that pretty much governed the remainder of his life – and miraculously, occasioned some of his best work. Do you see the problems a biographer had to face? Nothing about Philip K. Dick sits easily in the imagination. His life is a hell of a story, in every possible sense.

Divine Invasions is, therefore, a biography that no orthodox biographer would have attempted. And because of the quirky subject, quirks are inevitable in the biography. They're forgiveable because, well, Philip K. Dick is a special case. I take it that such trespass as Sutin takes is a side effect of sorting through Dick's own innumerable speculative self-analyses. At worst, what Sutin indulges in is nowhere near as silly as what, for example, Ernest Jones regularly gets into with his milestone biography of Freud. Also forgiveable, I suppose, are the cyberpunk chapter headings, and the invention of a special adjective – *phildickian* – to describe the unique intellectual trajectories of Dick's intelligence.

The most serious difficulty Sutin gets into, inevitably, is over those 1974 visions Dick had that effectively changed him from a crazy writer to a science mystic. Sutin was faced with the choice of trying to remain completely skeptical about the visions – and thereby gaining the illusion of objectivity – or of treating them as given phenomena, and thus taking the risk of being sucked into their dynamic. He chose the latter course, and managed, against the odds, to keep his head reasonably clear.

Sutin doesn't hide his admiration and love for Philip K. Dick the writer of books, the citizen, or the lunatic. The love keeps him from the futile exercise of trying to make the work and life add up to a coherent whole, which it doesn't. Personally, I was grateful that he didn't try, because in the late 20th century, those human lives that can be added up usually come to a negative balance. The real gifts of this biography are that it makes you like Philip K. Dick, and more important, it makes you want to read his books and see for yourself.

It sparked my interest strongly enough that I went back and reread three or four of the novels, and obtained several more I hadn't read before. I came away from the rereadings with renewed admiration for Dick. His ideas are usually sound, most have remained remarkably current, and his prose is mechanically even better than I remembered. I note in passing that only about a third of Dick's work is currently in print. Neither *Valis* nor *Ubik*, both among the best, are available. One of the extremely useful unorthodoxies in Sutin's study, incidentally, is a 20-page chronological guide to Dick's novels. Sutin has rated them on a 1-to-10 scale, and while I wasn't always in agreement with Sutin's evaluations, the listings will give newcomers a place to start.

Finally, I don't agree, as literary executor Paul Williams seems to say in the foreword to Sutin's biography, that Philip K. Dick should remain a cult figure whose books skitter along the outer margins of respectability. I'm very much from the Ed Sanders school, the one that doesn't enjoin current notions of literary respectability and despises cults and secrets. We've forgiven Dickens and Dostoyevsky for serializing their novels in the pulps. Why not forgive science fiction for its humble beginnings, and start the work of extracting the best?

Philip K. Dick should be placed directly in the literary and philosophical mainstream of 20th century literature. He was, quite bluntly, one of the English-speaking world's best writers of the post-war period. We should start acknowledging that.

Hungry Mind Review

THROUGH A
TESTOSTERONE-
SMEARED GLASS,
DARKLY

A woman I know in Vancouver – she's a feminist in her forties, tough-minded and politically smart – recently surprised everyone she knows by marrying the stumpish, bad-tempered, chronically silent troll she'd been dating for the previous several months. No one could figure out quite what the attraction was, and when I finally got up the courage to ask her, she came back with an interesting answer. She said that she'd realized he was unusual when he didn't talk about his mother on the first date. But she married him because he didn't ever complain about his poor, unappreciated male sexuality.

Somewhat obliquely, this little anecdote begins to explain what's wrong with Barry Callaghan's novel *The Way the Angel Spreads Her Wings*, which Canada's press with the highest overheads, Lester & Orpen Dennys, recently published. Had this novel been published in 1959, it might have been an important one. But times, mercifully, have changed. In 1989 it reads as yet another tired attempt to see and define the world through a testosterone-smeared glass, darkly.

The decades after World War II produced an abundance of novels that confused male sexuality with history and culture. Most were written under the influence of novelists like Ernest Hemingway, James Joyce, and toward the end of the period, Malcolm Lowry, which is to say, with guns and booze bookending a hyperactive philoprogenitive and other uniquely male glands. The apex of this genre, to my mind, appeared in Norman Mailer's *Advertisements for Myself*, most of which was written in the late 1950s. It was a failed novel that Mailer turned into a novella. He called it "The Time of Her Time," and it's an unintentionally hilarious sendup of the Hemingway mystique that chronicles the sexual exploits of an Irish-American would-be novelist who operates a bull fighting school in New York City.

Mailer's story, big surprise, doesn't have much to do with bullfighting. It is about what Barry Callaghan's novel is about: men who treat a violent, unjust world – and the women in it – as occasions for yet more blind, groaning, exploitative, torrential, male orgasms. The orgasms are interchangeably literary and sexual – and the orgasms are those ultimate, quintessential and universal meaning-of-life orgasms that mysteriously affirm everything, explain all, run over everything in their path and change absolutely nothing.

It seems like nearly everybody except a few male novelists over fifty has grown weary of being drenched by these self-affirming orgasms, and by all the cultural and political side-effects of permitting ten-second gender-specific neurophysical (and genetically superfluous) reactions to being rubbed the right way govern the fate of the species. Mailer's literary drenching is very specific about the subject of orgasms. Typically, his male protagonist has quite a few of them, and the novella's heretofore frigid female lead character eventually has one too, or so the story claims. But the point that everyone but the over-fifty novelists miss, and which no one else does these days, is that within the genre, everything is a prop for these fabulous male orgasms, be it bulls, guns, women, cities, even planets.

Barry Callaghan, of course, brings his own distinctively updated style and pathology to this conundrum. His protagonist is a morally exhausted Toronto-born photographer named, symbolically, Adam Waters. The novel's action traces Waters' desultory search for his childhood sweetheart and love-of-his-life Gabrielle O'Leary. He tracks her down in Puerto Rico, where she promptly disappears on him, and eventually to an unnamed but war-(and cliché-)torn African country where she is living in a leper colony. Waters also searches for her in his own sexual memory, and within a flashback Irish-Canadian booze-jazz-and-gravestone labyrinth of their respective parental relationships.

In his quest for the ultimate orgasm, Callaghan draws in several familiar icons. Sometimes it is Ponce de Leon's search for the fountain of youth, and at other times it is Conrad's Heart of Darkness. Neither the author or his narrator seem to be sure which it is. I guess this is called literary ambiguity. But I note that we never get a clear view of what Gabrielle really wants. About all we find out about her is that she has big breasts, big orgasms, long legs, and (to add some currently fashionable preoccupations) that she was molested by her choir-master father while she was a teenager.

For all the book's gushingly descriptive prose, we never quite get to the fine details of this woman, who is the only potentially compelling character in the story. We never discover her hair colour, and all we get about her eyes is that they're "almond" – whether this refers to their shape or colour isn't specified. She is really just a stage prop for Waters' sexual ego, anyway. Every conceptual and developmental difficulty in the book is focused on Waters' sexuality, and they get resolved – when they do – by the author's linguistic orgasms. At all the crucial moments where you'd expect a writer to be trying to imagine a new universe, Callaghan seems content to merely close his eyes, bear down on his writing implement, and, well, write harder. The real purpose of the novel, evidently, is to find male sexuality's inner station and unleash its orgasmic secrets. Or is it secret orgasms? And anyway, who cares?

It's fortunate that we don't, because we never really find out what the secret is. Part of the impediment lies with the way the book is written and organized. It needed a severe editing it didn't get. The first half of the book is littered with start-up debris, and the entire text is crowded with unbelievably silly dialogue counterpointed with long, mechanically inept sentences that somehow manage to sound like Hemingway and Lowry at the same time.

Melding those two styles might seem like a reasonable, if slightly antiquarian, accomplishment, but it isn't. The white characters talk like private detectives, and the Third Worlders all talk like Uncle Remus – and all the dialogue is constantly being marooned by typhoons of purple prose. In one of the African *Heart of Darkness* sequences, for instance, Waters encounters a German polka band playing in a humid bar, and is asked by a black hooker how he likes it.

> "Love it," he said, unbelievingly, and suddenly wished he had his cameras, because that was how he captured what he couldn't believe in, how he held on to all the lone solitary moments, stealing them in black and white from the blurred sheen of light that sometimes seemed to be all he could see, as if a flooding reality always hardened into walls of clear ice filled with light, light that blinded him.

Light is a repeated theme throughout, not unexpectedly. Light ought to be important to a photographer, of course, and that's what Adam Waters does for a living. You'd therefore expect the allusions to be competently technical, but instead what we get is all-too-frequent mystical allusions to its properties as a component of warfare, darkness, leprosy, Toronto and orgasms. They're not always illuminating or clear, and the brightest moments are, predictably, tied to Waters' will-to-orgasm, as in this rhapsodically over-written passage:

"The night air's always so damned clean when you're naked," she said and dove into the water and he dove after her, cutting swaths of light down through the water, their bodies rising to the surface, shouting, and they thrashed the water, smacking the heels of their palms against the water, driving sprays of light into their faces, beaded shawls streaming over their shoulders as they kissed, kissing droplets of light from their cheeks, trying to touch and raise bursts of light all over their bodies.

Some of the colourful prose would be tolerable if the book were better organized. The constant flashbacks, which are no doubt meant to be slightly disorienting, succeed all too well. In the novel's best passages, which depict a Kafkaesque Third World arrest-and-inter-rogation routine, the prose rises out of its self-stroking turgidity, and we see, briefly, the world Waters is trapped in, and which, presum-ably, Callaghan wants us to know about. Yet when Waters is re-leased, the tension created is totally dissipated by thirty pages of bor-ing flashbacks between the time he leaves the front steps of the police station and arrives in the parking lot where he has left his car.

By the time Callaghan's hero reaches the leper colony and has his last few orgasms with the heroine before she tells him to take a hike, you're kind of wishing the terrorists he's braved to get there had put him out of his misery. Ironically, Callaghan has already supplied the proper epitaph for his hero, and for the novel.

"'There's no perspective' he thought. 'Nowhere's everywhere, you swallow your own voice.'" Unfortunately, Callaghan didn't.

Globe and Mail

EAST VAN
ÜBER ALLES?

At the best of times, poetry anthologies are peculiar beasts. The editors and contributors don't always recognize that they're unicorns, dodos or carrier pigeons, but more and more, these anthologies seem like cultural equivalents of Noah's ark. This isn't the best of times for poetry, or, for that matter, for books and readers of any kind. The deluge isn't quite upon us, but these are, to use the Chinese expression, "interesting times". There are no longer any guarantees that any part of the human intellectual repertoire will survive them, let alone metaphor and the quaint little volumes of printed paper that for 500 years have been the working laboratories of metaphor.

At the best of times, poetry anthologies are attempts to secure the community traffic of what will remain, despite its lack of popularity, a fundamental human cognitive activity – the use of metaphor. Most of the anthologies that get published have become something considerably less than that, of course. Most are attempts to establish academic hegemonies, or are simply publishing projects taken on by publishers with axes to grind, or by university professors trying to legitimize their departmental programs or their personal tenure.

The last serious anthology published in Canada was Dennis Lee's 1986 M&S anthology of poets who began publishing between 1970 and 1985. Lee tried, with limited success, to evaluate the relative skills of the last generation of Canadian poets who have had the luxury of believing – without being certifiably braindamaged – that poetry is part of the cultural mainstream. Any poet (and any anthologist) nowadays must begin with the recognition that they and their craft are culturally marginal.

This condition doesn't exactly encourage and most of the poetry books and anthologies I've read in the last several years are either overreachingly silly, or just plain dull. When they aren't, it is a pleasant surprise.

East of Main: An Anthology of Poems from East Vancouver, edited by Calvin Wharton and Tom Wayman, is one of the pleasant surprises. First of all, it is a fun anthology. Much of it is readable and some of it pleasantly so. I can think of some poets who hang out in Vancouver's east side I would have included, such as Kevin Davies and Dorothy Trujillo. But there are always exclusions in anthologies, and the ones here are probably circumstantial. Maybe they were out of town, or pretending to be film projectionists, or pregnant. Young poets are also prone to obscure self-importances, and they fight among themselves a lot. In any case, Calvin Wharton and Tom Wayman were the editors, not me. Privately I was pleased to be able to read the work of several people I've been playing baseball against for the past several years, and still more pleased to discover that they're talented poets, and, har, har, that their language skills aren't a measure of their performance on a baseball diamond.

Just so it's clear where *I'm* coming from, I'll point out that I'm in the middle of a ten-year moratorium on publishing my own poetry. What that means is that I don't feel left out of this anthology even though I live in East Vancouver, and that I don't have any personal or theoretical axes to grind. I do, however, have some serious questions to ask about the anthology, and maybe about poetry anthologies in general. Most of the questions will concern the editorial structure and biases the editors have imposed, but the really important ones will be directed at the poets.

Let me begin the interrogation with the anthology's introduction. Editors Wharton and Wayman start off with the thoroughly contradictory but customary claims to both uniqueness and to international precedents. The impulse that created this anthology, they say, comes from a 1985 Australian anthology titled *Off the Record* that collected the writings of "work" writers, experimentalist chanters, poet-artists and feminist spokespersons instead of the usual denizens of poetry anthologies: college professors and their acolytes.

Having made this gesture, the editors felt compelled to expose the irrelevance of all other recent anthologies they know of. In the case of Vancouver's two other recent anthologies, both occasioned by Expo 86, they can proceed with considerable justification, even if they're mixing the aims of art with those of the tourist bureau – or confusing the quick with the braindead.

That seems to encourage them to get even sillier, and they propose that East Vancouver is the new centre of the poetic universe. This move – predictable as it is – is where they start to get into trouble. They're apparently undaunted by their own research logic, which, were it applied to 400 (or 4000) other centres of activity in Canada and the U.S., would expose the same phenomena: young, economically and culturally marginalized writers trying to crawl out from under the diseased but still hyperproductive poetic world of university-centred literature studies.

Finger pointing and manifesto manufacturing are lots of fun, but in a culture where no one at all is reading poetry except poets, it is really only a signal of an editorial schizophrenia that creates both an unaccounted-for bias and, worse, a debilitating rhetoric. We all shine on, right? But when the quality of the shining isn't contextualized, the result is usually just another unwanted product – and in this case, another group of poets twiddling their thumbs – uniquely, of course – while the civilization collapses around them.

I think there's a little more than that going on here, so let me give you some local history. *East of Main* is the offspring of two rather unlikely parents. One of them is poet Tom Wayman and an organization called the Vancouver Industrial Writers Union. Members of this group write sentimental Marxist poems that valorize the workplace and give us New Age slogans about smashing capitalism and various other evils. The other parent of *East of Main* is a group of poets, fronted here by Calvin Wharton, who have grown (to their credit) irritable with the touchy-feely internalizations of self and language that characterized the decay of the New American Poetry and the apolitical shenanigans of the Naropa Institute. Wayman's group is unhappy with the social and political injustices of contemporary society, and wants its poems to give vent to that unhappiness, while Wharton's group wants poetry to regain some formal and intellectual rigour. Both are admirable intentions.

What the two sides of this strange coalition share most consistently is a dislike of authority and a willingness to submit poetic composition to a set of theoretical principles that circumscribe aspects of composition. For the industrial poets, the circumscribed aspect is subject matter, which has to be about industrial accidents and the indignity of labour. Meanwhile, they seem satisfied to use whatever conventional forms of verse happen to be around. For the other group, subject matter hardly seems to matter. It is ordinary syntax – the communicative syntax of conversation or discourse – that is under interdiction.

As coalitions go, this should be a very uneasy one. Yet it doesn't appear to be. The radical (and usually socialist) values of both factions have long since mutated with the anti-authoritarian values all poets carry, and the obvious contradictions between the two groups have been subsumed in a collective – and often unexamined – contempt for the status quo wherever they perceive it. They resemble the rest of the left, actually, in that they're so enamoured of professional struggles – procedural and canonical – that they haven't noticed that a commercially globalist culture has sped right past them, leaving them in an intellectual and programmatically senile kabbala.

I happen to think that Wharton and Wayman are right when they say that the anthology is a signal of a cultural flowering of real interest and talent. Given that we understand that a cultural flowering of poets isn't a serious threat to the status quo, *East of Main* demonstrates the presence of a veritable hothouse of interesting writing.

No, that wasn't a typo in the last sentence. Like CanLit, *East of Main* is the product of a hot*house*, not a hot*bed*. Despite the posturing, these poets aren't growing potatoes for the masses and they aren't producing radical theory. The theory comes from the United States and Europe, and it is fifty years old. These are flowers they're cultivating – a different kind of flower, maybe, from those grown in the larger hothouse of UniversityLit, but ones that suffer from the same shortcomings that blight it – the chief being that nobody wants them.

The introduction to *East of Main* leaves me wondering if the editors understand this. They make a thoroughly silly and self-aggrandizing claim that the East Vancouver renaissance has occasioned a real estate boom. Somehow, according to them, the gradual influx of writers and painters into East Vancouver over the last twenty years has doomed it to an onslaught of developers' bulldozers and yuppie condominiums. The idea, apparently, is that the artists and writers are what have made the area attractive to developers – poets as antennae for the real estate industry.

I mean, get serious. There are one or two other factors involved, and it isn't quite time for the Ghost Dance. The truth of the matter is that East Vancouver is Vancouver's only neighbourhood where socially and economically marginal artists could possibly form a community. They have done so, and it's a reasonably nice place to live and write as a result, if you're an artist. But there's nothing unusual or noble about artists being forced to the margins of society. It's been like that for centuries, and if there's anything unique about the East Vancouver situation, it is the absurd fact that an anthology that announces its uniqueness also predicts its imminent demise.

East of Main is divided into three parts. The first contains poems *about* East Vancouver, the second, poems written *in* East Vancouver. Both these sections consist primarily of self-revelatory poems with conventional subject matter and diction, comprehensible to those few souls inclined or trained to read them. Mostly the poets write about how sensitive they are, and how awful the world is, but there is also some sophisticated celebration of life on the margin, fueled by the authors' rage, indignation and sorrow at social and political injustice.

The third section, however, is the *true* occasion for the anthology. It features poets from a movement called "language centred poetry" a.k.a. language centred writing (hereafter referred to as "LCW"). To explain this group of poems, Wharton and Wayman quote American poets Charles Bernstein, Ron Silliman and Bruce Andrews, the wise men three of LCW.

I'll give you their quotes, then offer translations. The quote from Bernstein tells us that LCW is "writing that takes as its medium, or domain of intention, every articulable aspect of language." Translation: *LCW poetry is about poets experiencing their language.* Silliman tells us that the "sum of the text is not reducible to any one of its statements." Translation: *You have to experience a poem, not merely summarize its meaning.*

Okay. I'm prepared to reject what my high school teachers taught me about reading poetry. But that's hardly revolutionary. So far, it hasn't even reached the outer limits of the William Carlos Williams/ Ezra Pound universe. Bruce Andrews, however, takes it a step further by saying that LCW "resembles a creation of a community and of a world-view by once-divided-but-now-fused Reader and Writer." As LCW goes, this statement is more suggestive of the movement's articulative technique than the other two. I'll try to translate it into plain English later, but right now I'm going to leave you alone to chew on it.

The editors' attempts to clarify what LCW is about aren't, unfortunately, very illuminating. They seem to know what LCW isn't, but are unable or unwilling to state clearly what it does do that other poetic methods haven't. Maybe they're afraid that some brontosaurus is going to stand up and say, "Well, isn't this just a super-complicated attempt to make poetry a public act without demanding that it also be socially interactive communication?" Of course I'd never offer such remarks, but the editors' inability to give a clear statement of the intentions of LCW makes me uneasy.

In any case, here's what the writing sounds like:

> Sometimes the subordinate clause is while you still have friends.
> Causality abets restless energy; ensues credit. If stool the
> size of an infant's head is removed from one's cadaver, it's a
> sign. Adjust connective degenerations. What appears to the eye
> and touch after twenty or thirty years is the same after forty
> or sixty, singing, cords, casts, stuck to the bottom.
>   (Deanna Ferguson, "Swoop Contract")

> Having had could supply the latches
> in a job-drought curriculum. Yet
> a proud and simple profile
> nods off with the voice
> of a pub noose....
>   (Jeff Derksen, "Grasping at Axles")

These randomly chosen passages – I could have quoted any or all of the work in the section – share a common characteristic. They're articulations of the self/language/world matrix that allows almost any response or interpretation. They're deliberately written in such a way that there's no specific meaning. The reader's interpretation of the poems – or rather, what they invoke in his or her language/self matrix – is theoretically of equal verity to whatever the authors have inscribed within them. Interpretation itself is unimportant, because the true subject is formal. The medium is the message, and that's what they confine the reader to thinking about. The result is a poetry of rather arid theoretical demonstration.

The legitimizing political element in LCW is its apparently non-authoritarian and anti-hierarchical nature. The authors record the signals and place them within the expressive medium, and you, as reader, do whatever you choose with them.

The trouble is that LCW begins and ends, it seems to me, with a betrayal of the artist's fundamental responsibility to communicate and to resist the alienation of meaning. It is a betrayal similar to that of the surrealists after the Great War. For the surrealists, the capitulation of responsibility was brought about by the technology-induced trauma of trench warfare, and the recognition that millions of human beings could be and were sacrificed to the hormonal and hegemonal dictates of a few senile generals, and to the greed of a corrupt political and banking system. LCW, in its turn, seems to be a capitulation brought about by the collapse of history and ideology in the face of Disney and the Global Village – a withdrawal into sentimental and free-floating labyrinths of the self from the recognition that our civilization and most of its subsystems are on a terminal trajectory.

Please don't mistake what I'm saying here. LCW *is* philosophically securable and at times, technically fascinating – as theory. The questions I'm directing at the *East of Main* poets are these impolite ones: So what? As an exemplary *artistic* behaviour, where does LCW lead? What kind of world does it project, and what elements of the existing human and natural community will it protect or enhance?

It seems to me, some seventy or so years after the emergence of surrealism, that what legitimized surrealism wasn't its theoretical tenets or the aesthetic artifacts it generated, which were frequently frivolous and second-rate. What made it interesting was the array of intellectual and imaginative tools others created to supplant its depressing testimonies. Two examples of what I mean are Walter Benjamin's fine-tuning of Marxism into a coherent and unsentimental socialistic aesthetic method, and Jean-Paul Sartre's psychologically workable antidote to the philosophical paralysis created by the Great War and the subsequent (and unexpected) reification of capitalism as fascism.

By itself, surrealism was a symptom, a howl of pain and outrage at a system of human relationships and ideas that had defied and defiled life itself. That's why Benjamin and Sartre were interested in it. I'm worried that among surrealism's post-nuke equivalents is LCW. That's fine if the poets involved are content to be merely skinhead symptoms of the current nihilist malaise. But the poets in *East of Main* strike me as too interesting and intelligent to settle for that.

Let's go back to Bruce Andrews' statement that LCW "resembles a creation of a community and of a world-view by once-divided-but-now-fused Reader and Writer." His sentence begins with a weaseling verb. To "resemble" a community is to assert nothing except appearance. Following this, Andrews refuses to use definite articles, and employs grammatical and case rhetorical embellishments without saying what kind of community or world view is involved. The effect is to create a syntactic and semantic wobble that virtually forces the reader to make a sentimental or teleological (or partisan) interpretation of what he means.

In effect, the sentence means anything the reader wants, provided the reader has the apocalyptic sensibility to want to read *through* it in the first place. It also denies the inherent sociality of language by deliberately refusing to be exact. Unkindly translated, it might mean that *LCW is a device based on a rhetorical unification of the communicator and the target of communication so as to give both the outward appearance of egalitarian community and intellectual coherence without any of the responsibilities of either community or coherence.* The LCW proposition that the reader and writer are fused manages to be nihilistic, totalitarian and apocalyptic at the same time. More depressing still, whatever community it proposes is linked by a kabbalarian syntax. Another stinking lousy secret society, in other words.

A community of private realities connected only by a secret syntax – and a sneakily authoritarian one at that, because the authority here is lodged in a theoretical base outside the poems – is a nihilistic one that extends the alienation we already suffer from. It may be an understandable reaction, this nihilism, given that the economic and social mainstream of our culture is based on the manipulation of information and commodities – on lying, exclusion, and trickery.

But in the end, it is reactionary and it will lead to more despair. The only community LCW can generate is one based on sharing the *impossibility* of shared experience. Given this, how could it even try to create an open community that carries an alternative to the secret elites and kabbalas that control most of our civilization? LCW is, therefore, not a community at all, but like surrealism before it, a reaction, a symptom. The frightening part is that it draws its energies from militating against the difficulties of discourse, the non-inclusive, wart-ridden processes of speech and writing upon which all human communities are based.

Kabbalarian syntaxes, which are at the root of any secret coding of phenomena, gain their power by exclusion. You're either in or you're out, you're either hip to the syntax or you aren't. Semantics, by contrast, is inclusive. It refers to discourse, which is too complex to secure and make exclusive because part of it is always going on outside the syntactic boundaries. The object of a semantic exercise isn't to render order, but to educate – to keep people talking in the midst of difficulty and contradiction. At its best it is an orderly but inherently dynamic caressing of complexity carried out with the existential recognition that no discourse can ever be complete – or perfectly satisfying.

That's a pretty accurate model for the way human intelligence works. Kabbalas and secret societies, whatever conditions occasion and energize them, are more or less the opposite. They are attempts to exclude – and when their members start wearing uniforms and carrying guns, to exterminate – whatever they can't control.

What I've noted above are just concerns and suspicions about which I'd be delighted to be proven wrong. I really don't have any militant conclusions to make about the individual writers featured in *East of Main*, except to say that talented as they are, the *East of Main* poets seem to be far too fucked up on certainty for their own good. LCW is another matter. It's interesting enough as a theoretical principle, but its uncommunicativeness makes it of dubious value as a long-term practice. It'll probably destroy what little audience poetry has left.

Instead of this cavilling conclusion, how about a confession? I quit publishing my own verse because what I was able to do within the medium didn't solve certain problems I've come to believe poetry has to solve if it is to be a viable artistic medium. Let me list my operating assumptions and the problems I couldn't solve.

Poetry, like any other artform, has to be public communication. A poetic line (or poem) should be a transfer of information that embodies the most efficient possible linguistic rendering of the passage of phenomena and ideas that doesn't ignore or lose the complexity of the passage. So far, so good. All decent poetry has always done that. But I want it to do more. It should also:

1. hold onto more of the evident social and phenomenal particularities of a cybernetics-driven culture than the old forms allow for. The retreat into expressive kabbalas killed the New American Poetry twenty years ago. Creating syntactic kabbalas is no better. It isn't an adequate response, politically or in any other sense, to the massive and systematic deceptions and manipulations of contemporary life that are being perpetrated all around us. We've got too many secrets and codes as it is.

2. change the old private soul at the public wall to phenomenally and/or intellectually ordered matrices of images, probably emanating from a sound/video studio. It's one thing to communicate inti-

mately from one person to another, and another to communicate from one end of the village to the other. In a global community, poetry should do both.

3. be more interesting – i.e. amusing in the sense Rimbaud intended when he characterized the Muse as a vampire who demands to be entertained. Right now, it's hard to argue that *any* poetry is doing this, be it CanLit, work poetry, or LCW.

Obviously, I can't yet make poetry do the things I'm demanding it do. But I'm convinced that they have to be done, and I have the uneasy feeling that LCW is a step in the wrong direction, or in no direction at all.

Vancouver Review

AUTISTS, ARTISTS, AND THE NEW NEUROLOGICAL CRITICISM

In a recent Globe and Mail review of a new Ezra Pound biography, novelist David Gurr suggested that Mr. Pound, Pablo Picasso, and if memory serves me, James Joyce, each suffered from neurological abnormalities, and that this, in part, was the source of both their creativity and their eccentric and frequently rotten personal behaviour. Although Gurr doesn't come out and say it directly, what he is implying is that Pound, Picasso and Joyce weren't really artists at all, but rather *autists*. No, Mr. Gurr does not have a lisp, and he isn't trying to pretend that he's from New York City. He's speculating that the creativity of artists is merely a side effect of neural abnormalities or anomalies that shut them out of conventional social reality and inside agnosial systems of perception.

Such an explanation of creativity is, of course, somewhat reductive, but there's nothing new about reductive theories of creativity. Twenty years ago it was fashionable to explain unusual behaviours, including creativity, as a result of poor potty training. The current mania for ascribing biochemical causes for everything from mass murder to hangnails is, if anything, an empirical improvement. At least now people want to blame neurology, not their parents, for their problems. What was more interesting – even remarkable – about the review was that Gurr has given the *Globe and Mail* a leg up on an ascendant school of literary criticism. In Canada, this school may soon eclipse the one that is grounded in Mr. Frye's notions of literature as Middle-Class Splendour in the Wilderness Surrounding the University of Toronto Campus, and it might even dislodge the self-referential linguistic relativism of deconstruction (a.k.a. the dance of Charles De Gaulle's nephews) that is dominant in many of our other universities. I'm entirely serious when I say that I believe David Gurr is onto something with an uncommon grain of good sense to it, not to mention excellent market potential. Such a combination of good sense and market potential should prove irresistible.

As an environment for critical exploitation, neurology is almost perfect. The human brain is the black box of modern medicine, and in this century has spawned a truly amazing array of symptom-centred technologies aimed at manipulating "normative" properties or reducing asymmetrical phenomena. With the demonstrable failure of the therapy-oriented disciplines that dominated the first three quarters of this century – psychology and psychoanalysis – neurology has emerged in the last ten years as the industry's logical frontier. It is also, arguably, among the last ones we have available to exploit.

The present state of neurology itself is downright fascinating. First of all, it operates from a very peculiar data-base. What we know about the architecture of the human brain is roughly equivalent to what we knew about Africa around 1700. We have a map of the coastline, and we have some information about what happens when brief, armed forays are made into the interior – strange things are discovered, local populations (of cells or natives) die in vast numbers or are transformed into automatons with new occupations. And all the while, the explorers speak of dark mysteries and dream of further profits.

Where the human brain is concerned, there are obvious reasons for the lack of exploration, of course. The brain is the control unit for the human body, and the documented interventions made thus far into operating ones have been tentative, clumsy, frequently fatal, and best carried out under authoritarian police regimes. Our conception of "normative" functioning process in the brain remains rudimentary, and by and large the treatment of neurological dysfunction is grounded on asserting dubious cultural norms or on supporting paradigmatic social modeling so general that it yields a vast and fuzzy pathological boundary – and nothing else save a lot of former experimental modules that stare at walls and drool.

The result is that it is the *diagnosis of pathology* which has created the working database. It is an almost totally theoretical and symptomatic database, equivalent in its veracity to describing the workings of an internal combustion engine by observing occasional spots of oil leaking from it or by attempting to fuel it with different substances – gasoline, Pepsi, cow's milk, etc. The established practice of attempting to tune the brain back into "normality" by crude surgical intervention aimed at disabling the offending parts or by administering convulsive drugs and massive electric shocks indicates that both the diagnostic and treatment apparatuses are about as sophisticated as Neanderthal pebble tools.

Oliver Sacks, who is certainly neurology's most entertaining practitioner and, somewhat revealingly, among its most prestigious, is probably the accidental source of Gurr's new cross-discipline application. He's written several readable books on the subject of neurological disorders. The best of them, *The Man Who Mistook His Wife for a Hat*, even became a bestseller a few years ago. Sacks' analyses of the various forms of neurological dysfunction is seductive – probably intentionally. Scrupulously acknowledging the field's poverty of data, and pointing to the inherent difficulties of extending the database, Sacks divided his bestseller into four neat categories – losses, excesses, transports, and a miscellaneous category that picks up "productive" anomalies like idiot savants and autistic visual and musical geniuses. Sacks illustrates each category with a series of anecdotal case histories. Some are chilling, some sad, and others are embarrassingly funny. Almost all are thought-provoking. Therein lies the problem.

This is, after all, the age of the entrepreneur, and entrepreneurism has concatenated with our artistic and scientific communities as much as anywhere else. Neurology, because it has a black box at its core, is perfect material for the intellectual entrepreneur. All one has to do is attach one's intellectual contraption to the promising lead-ins that trail from the neurological black box, and *shazam!!!* a new explanation for reality can be generated without much fear that a real expert will refute it. Hard to, when no real experts exist.

I ran into David Gurr shortly after his *Globe and Mail* review of the Pound biography came out, and I slyly asked him if he'd been reading Oliver Sacks. He realized instantly that I was teasing him, and replied gruffly that he'd read more than just Sacks. He didn't say exactly what he'd been reading, but no matter. Despite his weakness for wearing seersucker leisure suits, Gurr is clearly a man of honour, so I accept his word on it – along with his assurances that what is implied in his review "is considerably more complicated than it might appear."

It's true that a number of competent artists have been investigating neurology for some time. Christopher Dewdney, who is Canada's most innovative poet, has been exploring neurology as a metaphorical model and parallel to larger biospheres for several years. The results, some of them lodged in his recent book *The Immaculate Perception*, are spectacular.

What is now going to happen, unfortunately, is unlikely to operate by Dewdney's high standards. Neurology as a metaphor for other systems is fine. Treating neurological abnormalities as the governing energy behind human creativity is dangerous.

Gurr seems to have placed his bet on artists as autists. That certainly coincides with the current view of artists as self-concerned and irresponsible jerks locked inside universes of artifice, subversion, kinky sex and god knows what other abnormal and antisocial activities. Personally, I'm putting my money on Tourette's syndrome, a dysfunction that runs the range of cognitive hyperactivity from creative hyper-alertness to ticked-out drooling. The best artists I know all demonstrate the induced tics of data overload – leading of course to a self-referential universe of artifice, subversion *et al.*

Even for the skeptical intellectual entrepreneur, other neural abnormalities will clear up a host of minor mysteries. No doubt all the terrible poetry being written could be explained as a symptom of tonal and cognitive agnosia. Or is it some new form of aphasia? Margaret Atwood's heretofore mysterious two-tone speech dysfunction will be explained as neural dysphonia. And Irving Layton is suddenly explainable – and slightly more attractive – as a marginal Tourette's, while Leonard Cohen's lyric delivery will find new categorization as intermittent catatonia.

The downside is that neurological criticism will probably re-energize CanLit Studies, and the old warhorses will now serve as easy material for academic reprocessing until at least the millennium. Damn. I thought they were about to drift off into encephalitic amnesis . . .

Books in Canada

PROLEGOMENA TO THE DEFENESTRATION OF JOHN BENTLEY MAYS

Neither Canada nor its artistic community breed many good right-wing liberal thinkers, which is surprising because most Canadian literati are right-wing liberals who pretend to be left-wing anarchists. We have a tradition of importing our good right-wing liberals, but lately the importation appears to have become wholesale, especially in the multidisciplinary avant garde centred around Toronto's A-Space, Vancouver's Western Front and a cross-country network of "alternate" galleries. There are times when these galleries seem more like asylums for the media-struck than a true avant garde. An interesting example of this is John Bentley Mays, who is connected with the gallery network, and acts as one of the editors of *Open Letter*, which has evolved as a primary organ of the network.

Mays appears to be an American refugee in search of a country Richard Grossinger hasn't yet deluged with his elegantly written and printed, ah, *sense impressions*. Credit Mays for recognizing a good thing when he sees one. Canada is the nearest English-speaking potential victim for Americans, and its artists are, relatively speaking, generously subsidized by the government. Thus, we have acquired John Bentley Mays, and quite a few more lesser lights who resemble him.

Open Letter has now published several articles and reviews by Mays. One of them, "Prolegomena to the Study of Daphne Marlatt," proves, among other things, that Mays is hip enough to have read the titles of Jane Ellen Harrison's books on Greek mythology. Mays' essay frolics through what he must have believed is relevant on the west coast writing scene to his urbane and capricious sensibility. The fragmentary erudition on the essay makes it sort of entertaining, but it didn't have much to do with the work of Daphne Marlatt. That, of course, may have had something to do with the opaqueness of Marlatt's work, which is a confusion of politically correct ideas, run-on sentences, and a narrative voice that somehow always manages to sound like it is lost – or better, bereft – in a windstorm.

Mays' recent *Open Letter* essay, entitled "Hobbes Body: Politics as Poetics" is, however, one I take violent exception to. It isn't just because Mays has decided he's Norman O. Brown or because he has stuffed his prose with pointless verbal complexities (for "coherent speech is the signative representation of the circuit of regulated thought" read "clear speech comes from clear thinking" – equally thunderous phrasings abound). Any contemporary interest in Hobbes warrants an alertness on the part of readers. Hobbes is the intellectual godfather of western capitalist democracy. Hannah Arendt, in *The Origins of Totalitarianism*, described Hobbes as "the only great thinker who ever attempted to derive public good from private interest and who, for the sake of private good, conceived and outlined a Commonwealth whose basis and ultimate end is accumulation of power."

What Mays does is apply Hobbes' logical arguments for the accumulation, distribution and application of political and economic power to art. Hobbes argued that the body politic could be resecured through a process of giving over political and social rights to a representative oligarchy, thus relieving the individual of social burdens and enabling him to get his shit together to pursue his own self-interest. Mays redefines the body politic as the elements and phenomena of imagination – a capricious definition, to say the least – and then argues that the apparent incoherence and multiplicity of the elements and phenomena must become subservient to the mastery of the "together" artist, who then presumably will be free to pursue the best interests of his or her career. Confused? Hell, it gets worse. He then goes on to say we must return to the natural, bodily sources of being through art in order to energize both personal life and art (he's apparently uninterested in the fate of anything else). What is good for the body politic is good for the self, he implies, because all erotic impulses are pure.

If all of this sounds like the erotic morality going down about 1966 when guys were running around using every text from the Bible to Kahlil Gibran to coerce their sexual target-of-preference into the sack, I can't help it. Such is the argument of John Bentley Mays and Thomas Hobbes in all its glory: "For it is the Unity of the Representer, not the Represented, that maketh the Person One."

To see what Mays really means, we have to go deeper into the opus of Hobbes. Hobbes, first of all, hadn't the slightest interest in making the world whole again. He was interested simply and only in the methods of creating social and political power. If we go back a little on him we discover that the idea of time and history as a circular or elliptical process was broken by about 1640, when Descartes provided the methodology for legitimizing the primacy of personal cosmology. Hobbes, in his turn, provided the method for cashing in on the fragmentation of the old cosmology and body politic. *Leviathan* provided the complete ethical basis for bourgeois society and for capitalism.

Mays, in his reading, makes the ignorant but not very surprising mistake of thinking that a pathology of imagination is the same thing as a conscious and socially responsive will and purpose. It isn't surprising because he is operating without a working concept of the social. He lands himself therefore in a solipsistic visionary state, the results of which would no doubt resemble what conventionally acceptable poetry has been by and large since Shelley. It psychologizes the real, encloses it within the oscillating boundaries of an egotism, and it leads to the kind of artistic half-life in which a Lewis Carroll and George Macdonald could sip tea on English country lawns and write of the wonders of childhood while seven-year-old children chained to industrial looms were beaten to death for crying at the darkness of the night.

I think art ought to do precisely the opposite of what it has been doing. It has to resume the prophetic role in which its imaginations see into the essential nature and specific acts of their epoch instead of aggrandizing the egos of the artists. Great art speaks neither in nor to the personal. The self, which does have a role in art, is simply the reflexive temporal and spatial focus through which that art informs us of the external.

John Bentley Mays argues that if natural (read "infantile") human motivations imitate nature-at-large then the collective social, political, and artistic activities should recapitulate both. In saying that he is once again failing to respect the distinction between pathology and rational purpose. He's also ignoring about 6000 years of human history, the positive side of which mostly documents our collective attempts to improve upon nature and to reduce its violence. These attempts to improve on nature, and the human communities that have emerged from the achieved improvements have had at least two purposes that bear on this argument: on the one hand the need for protection from natural and human violence, and on the other the eugenic fact that exclusive sexual activity within one's own genetic boundaries eventually makes folks sterile or gives them two heads and more digits than you can comfortably stick inside a baseball glove or a pair of shoes.

Ultimately, self-interest, however "enlightened", is now and always has been a genteel excuse for the strong and powerful to go on exploiting the weak, the ignorant and the innocent. Bourgeois society, while it has succeeded in making the exploitation that is pretty well universal more diffuse and indirect, can't alter its fundamental mode of operation any more than Marxist governments can hide their own rigid stupidity. I'm amazed that anyone today can still regard the world as an occasion for willful self-indulgence and self-interest – especially given the record of the last 150 years and the now highly visible effects of having our best minds sitting in country gardens discussing utility and personal technology while two thirds of the people in the world are chained to the looms of progress. Doing so involves a denial of the value of those limited egalitarian institutions created by human societies – institutions which, despite their faults, have been successful in resisting the violence and expedience of nature. The fact that bourgeois society does imitate nature in its economic and political forms can't now be and never should have been regarded as an acceptable moral rationale for continuing. As we overpopulate and pollute this planet, those human improvements on nature – the egalitarian sociopolitical and economic institutions created to keep us from practicing self interest – will have to gain increasing importance. They will, in simple truth, become the basis for the survival of the species and of nature itself.

I have, then, two messages. The first is that tiny balkan nations like our own ought to beware of people who think and write like John Bentley Mays. The phenomenal world and the sweet procedures of imagination are more than occasions for a career in creative writing.

The second message is a more difficult and crucial one, having to do with acceptable freedoms within art. Octavio Paz points out somewhere that while bourgeois society may offer us various kinds of freedom, the freedoms gained are suspect. Because it is based on the exploitation of human beings by human beings, bourgeois society is dedicated to the denial of freedom.

After all the liberation that has been the social substance of the last twenty years – sexual liberation, the increased distance most of us now live from raw subsistence – there are only two freedoms that seem worth pursuing and having: freedom from human exploitation and abuse by other human beings, and the freedom to develop and educate one's own faculties. And I can't get around the notion that we can't educate ourselves while we are being manipulated and lied to. Otherwise it's every man for himself, John Bentley Mays, our common chains, and crying in the night beneath the humming machinery of the new cybernopolis.

NMFG

ROBIN MATHEWS
AND THE
LANGUAGE
OF IRE

Most of the people I hang around with laugh nervously whenever Robin Mathews' name comes up. They speak about him – always briefly – as if he were a kind of intellectual pitbull with rabies and no leash, and then insist on talking about something else. Anything else.

I happen to think that Robin Mathews is an interesting figure who needs to be understood and explained. He doesn't require excuses and he doesn't deserve to be laughed at. As an academic at Carleton University he's been a leading figure in the fight against the Americanization of Canadian universities, and he has been active within the radical left for years. He's not a kook, and you know he isn't because kooks are generally treated with tolerance. Mathews draws the antagonism and even hatred of a surprising number of people, and the thoughtless ill-will of a lot more people who should be sympathetic. His unfortunate tendency to attack personalities sometimes blurs what he has to say, but given his understanding of what is at stake – the cultural and political survival of Canada – that's a forgivable if not exactly charming fault. At close range, incidentally, Robin Mathews is a remarkably nice person, one who is always up for a polite argument. Really.

Unfortunately, he also writes books. *Language of Fire*, from Steel Rail Publishing, is one that provides, one suspects, a rather clear measure of Mathews' cherished ideas, and his literary talent at expressing them. The book is a confusion of surprisingly traditional intellectual and emotional habits grappling with the most profound political and intellectual issues of our time. His approach to poetry is therefore somewhat contradictory. At the same time as he is demanding that poetry become more sensitive to material reality, he uses precisely the technical conventions that have drawn poetry into the seclusion and privacy it has fallen to.

He's a poet of several voices, and they aren't very well integrated. The lyric voice in his verse keeps on dropping lines like *Fall fields and air are funnells flying free*, and most often the poems sound like they escaped from a suburban poetry circle that got lost in the closet in the 1930s. He tries to keep this almost embarrassed voice apart from the other poems, and apart from his ideas about political revolution and social injustice, as if he found its presence a little unfortunate but unavoidable – or as if his academic training has led him to write that way, if only to show he's human.

The second voice in the book is a kind of voice almost no reader of poetry wants to hear. It is an ideologically strident leftist voice. One of its few moments of humour – possibly unintentional – is worth repeating:

> The opposite of love is hate. The opposite of clarity is hate
> expressed through action, taking rather than giving. When our
> Yankee friends want to spread the American way of life, they
> mean they want everyone to agree to their system of looting the
> world. Looting at home is called "Capitalism". Looting around the
> world is called "Imperialism".

Yeech, giggle, giggle. Most people will simply turn off when they come to this kind of language, knowing vaguely where it is coming from even if they haven't bothered to find out anything about how it sees the world. Mathews would call this rejection "the rationalization by the oppressed classes of their condition" and he would be right, but no one will listen to that either. Most of Mathews' poems are a kind of ungainly hybrid of journalism, pedagogy and poesy that has more of the weaknesses than the strengths of each. Its failure is that it rarely breaks through the cultural defences readers will throw up against it.

The sad truth is that the alienated working class isn't listening to poetry because there's nothing for them in it and because they don't know how to listen. And anyway, they prefer television. Some parts of the middle classes still read poetry, but are thrown into confusion by descriptions of reality that hold collective values as the highest good. To confuse readers further, Mathews' voice shifts from invective to humour to clear common sense, and it is constantly undercut by his rage at and hostility to his intended audience. And though this anger has been richly earned through the mistreatment he's received from the academic world in this country, it isn't very helpful if you're trying to listen to him.

Mathews raises a third voice in the book. It is the least evident and the most interesting one, and while I'm prepared to argue that readers ought to struggle with the second because it is full of information, it is this other voice that keeps grabbing at me as I read him. The voice is really that of William Wordsworth, that wonderful, repressed patriarch. The love-objects have changed and they don't have the clarity or constancy they had for Wordsworth, but they're there and so are the cadences. The best moments in *Language of Fire* sound like this:

O man, look down this street
where men and women follow hot machines
sweating out profit for the Lords of Brass

and growing hard past sweetness or fair hope –
here's beauty for a lifetime's work.
Lift up those hearts.

That most of Mathews' poems are either rabidly polemic or stuffed
with silliness about the snowflakes in Ottawa is not the point. Sure,
Mathews is an easy mark for any cynical wit who needs to put him
down. I guess I'd have to say those people most of all should listen to
him. Mathews has a quality of passionate vulnerability in the face of
the milieu he emerges from – the rugged and brainless individualism
of our economic and cultural tradition – that offers a vision of human
life in which people – lots of people – need and could have decent
lives. I don't see his hatred of stupid misery or his interest in people
often among writers these days. Mathews shares that quality with
Milton Acorn, who wrote a really supercilious and dumb introduction to the book that demonstrates another quality both men share: an
inability to keep their eye on the ball.

As Marxists, both are all too willing to declare the monstrousness
of capitalism without paying any attention to the fact that the monster
is an enemy to art for different reasons than it is an enemy of Marxism's beloved revolutionary working classes. Capitalism needs to
disperse social and intellectual energy in order to foster the competition and productivity that ensures its continuance. Art tends to integrate ideas and phenomena, and is therefore a minor but real hostile
force within a capitalist economy and social order. That's why Plato
wanted it out of his republic, and it's why poetry has been shunted
from the public arena over the last century or so into a realm of private self-expression where it can dovetail harmlessly with the ethical
screen of the power structure – or can simply bounce off it into the
gutter. In our time poetry is regarded by the governments of the capitalist democracies as a genial form of unemployment, or a poufter's
hobby.

The inability to keep their eye on the ball leads both Mathews and
Acorn to an aggravating brand of personification in which, for

instance, Raymond Souster is the symbol of colonial passivity and Charles Olson symbolizes American cultural imperialism. Canadian passivity towards American cultural imperialism is a real and specific danger, not something that can be transferred wholesale to particular figures in national and international poetry.

In my experience, American poets – wherever they're living – are at least as alienated as those in Canada. Charles Olson, for all his nattering about the power he had at Gloucester city hall, and his monomaniacal claims late in life that he understood the powers that control this world, doesn't deserve to be personified as a cultural monster. Moreover, many of the Americans living and working as artists in this country have become exemplary citizens, and ought to be judged for what they do, not for where they came from. Olson's influence has been a positive force for Canadian culture, because he argued on behalf of the particular and the local, and didn't much care on which side of the border it occurred. When Americans play Pax Americana – and some do – they aren't good citizens. But they're a relatively minor element of American imperialism and shouldn't be mistaken for the beast itself.

What Mathews doesn't seem to understand is that cultural life isn't the same as political life. The boundaries and structures of culture are more mixed up in the vagaries of personal history and traditions that no one, on the whole, knows much about because we've been inside them all our lives. At the same time, culture is interpenetrated by ideas that cross national boundaries more easily than political ideas do, and for that we should be grateful rather than paranoiac. By applying Mathews' logic, one would conclude that the influence of Karl Marx himself is a dangerous form of cultural imperialism. Personally, I think there's a better case for Marx and Lenin as cultural imperialists than for Charles Olson or Rainer Maria Rilke.

Instead of trying to chase out foreign devils, Mathews and other cultural nationalists should be insisting that any idea or structure of thought be applied with a clear knowledge of local conditions. Few artists are interested enough in ideas to do this, particularly when the ideas are related to questions of how human beings should or do live their lives. But Mathews, as a Marxist, is interested in ideas. Unfortunately, most Marxists spend so much time dithering about the correctness of their ideological stance that they don't know their assholes from their back yard.

Ironically, this all leaves me wishing that Mathews was a better poet. The cultural power poetry once had lies in the passionate specificity and thoroughness of its perception of reality. Fighting to regain that power and demanding that poets work toward this goal would be a useful demand Mathews could make. He doesn't, because of his righteousness and because he keeps on seeing American poets as the enemy. Nor does he give any indication that poets might provide us all with a language that doesn't merely stack everyone on the side they're already on.

Marxism, as Sartre has argued from within the left, has never had a language or a phenomenology that could account for the complexity of the human organism. For reasons Marxist analysis doesn't account for, human experience, while it occurs within history and its determinants, has now been recognized as having other, equally powerful determinants. Many of these determinants are cybernetic and technological complexities that tend to crush both historical perspective and personal autonomy. Marxists deny the existence of any other kind of experience than that which has been dialectically determined by the Marxist view of history when they have been developing more sophisticated models of class relations. In the wealthier industrialized states, where subsistence is mainly just an indirect threat in people's lives, the difficulties human beings suffer (and share) is this confusing complexity – and the fragility of the human organism it reveals.

The left, in art at least, seems determined to pretend that the complexity of contemporary existence has no relation to history, preferring a pedagogy organized around the economic and social determinants and language of the 19th century. Yet the role is there for poetry to become useful again, and the tools are there in the trade if not in the tradespeople themselves.

I don't know if Robin Mathews is capable or even interested in what that role might lead to, but *Language of Fire* is closer to the problems poets should be facing than most of the poetry one reads. And so is Robin Mathews. I just wish he was a better writer, and that his personal rancour would ease enough to make him a more open thinker.

NMFG

WHO ARE
THE ENEMIES
OF CULTURE?

Some years ago Norman Mailer related an anecdote about an interview he'd done for one of the large radio networks. The interviewer, posing as a fellow radical, encouraged Mailer to make some reasonably inflammatory statements, and Mailer cheerfully complied. The content of that interview, however, is and was incidental. The real substance was technical. After the interview was completed, the interviewer reworked the interview tape in the studio, rerecording his own voice to make it seem tonally richer than it was, and subtly altering many of the questions to make Mailer's responses appear more extreme than they were. The only apology the interviewer made, when Mailer asked for an explanation, was that the tape recorder's batteries had been defective, thereby necessitating the rerecording of the interviewer's voice. The interviewer never did admit to distorting the substance of the interview.

Recently, I've had the misfortune of having much the same thing done to me in Vancouver bookseller and CanLit entrepreneur William Hoffer's publication of a private correspondence between the two of us. Published under the rather revealing imprint of the Final Judgement Construction Co., the 23-page pamphlet is an example of intellectual and scholarly bad faith worthy of Mailer's yellow journalist/interviewer. The difference is that in Hoffer's case, the initial (and ultimate) defects are in the glorious CEO of the Final Judgement Construction Co., not in a tape recorder's batteries. Hoffer revised his part of the correspondence, added a letter that I never received, and deleted at least one hysterical and incoherent letter he did mail to me. He does not appear to have edited my part of the correspondence, except to make one or two careless typos that weren't in the originals, but he did make the rather silly editorial gesture of printing my letters in a noticeably smaller, sans serif typeface.

At issue in the correspondence are three more or less separate items. One of them, which Hoffer doesn't acknowledge in his editing of the correspondence, is that he's angry at me because he thinks I sabotaged his attempt to enter the field of literature in a new role. He's been writing in the privacy of his closet for many years, but I had the misfortune to be present when he unleashed, for the scrutiny of some other writers in an informal workshop, some new pieces of writing. One of the pieces was a story about killing a dog, written from the point of view of the four- or five-year-old male child who conspired, very skillfully, to have the dog put down. Along the way, Hoffer's child/narrator gave evidence of having read Marx and Hegel, and the story was transparently and awkwardly autobiographical. Hoffer also submitted a number of poems to the group, at least one of them written directly at me. None of his literary efforts are very important here, except to note that I have a mean streak when it comes to people who are cruel to animals, and that Hoffer did not, in publishing the correspondence, offer his literary efforts for further public scrutiny.

The second item concerns Hoffer's lack of intellectual scruples, and the irrational and unethical ethics he exhibits in publishing the correspondence without permission. One might excuse his misbehaviour as side effects of his personal health problems, or ascribe them to his dependence on peculiar vitamins. I won't do that. I've chosen to terminate our always-rocky personal association, and I have taken my book business elsewhere as well.

The third item, and the only really important one, concerns the differing cultural politics within the published correspondence. The motive behind the "cultural offensive" Hoffer outlines in his part of the correspondence is, as far as I understand it, grounded in a desire to see all government subsidies to cultural activities removed. He's focused his paramilitary venom on the most visible source of subsidy to the arts, the Canada Council. He wants the subsidies taken from Canadian publishers, and the subsistence grants taken away from Canadian writers. Presumably he would have all our other cultural industries treated the same way.

His attitude toward the universities, which are a less obvious recipient of artistic subsidy in Canada, is considerably more ambiguous. This is probably because a very large part of his business income derives from the university libraries around the country, and he doesn't want to bite the hand that feeds him. During the time that this correspondence went on, for instance, he was in the process of negotiating, cataloguing and selling CanLit archival materials belonging to several prominent Vancouver authors to either the university libraries or the National Library in Ottawa, or both.

Cutting all the existing subsidies, Hoffer seems to be arguing, will cause a kind of literary Armageddon in which the "real" writers will rise to the surface and function in neocapitalist entrepreneurial splendour. The "unreal" writers, presumably, will dissolve into the little puddles of effete slime he believes them to be, to be ground beneath the boots of Hoffer's new free-enterprising literary superpersons. If that description contains mixed metaphors and is disturbingly military in its imagery, don't blame me. Hoffer talks like that. So far he has been noticeably short on specific proposals about what should happen to those "unreal" writers who do not cooperate with his declaration of war except that they will be, in his eyes, war criminals.

My own proposals, as contained in what I thought was going to be a confidential and exploratory correspondence, were admittedly not entirely coherent either. In that respect, I guess I'm a little grateful to Hoffer for making me think them through more carefully, and therefore I don't entirely object to his publication of the correspondence. I do regret several offhand remarks I made about several Vancouver writers, but only because the remarks were unkind, and in shorthand. In it, I said that I don't think that now-deceased D.M. Fraser was a very important writer, and I'll stick with that judgment. I *do* think that Jon Furberg could be a very important poet if he got rid of his fear of working in any other mode than the ecstatic/elegiac. Likewise, I am generally critical of writers who drink or use drugs as a means of avoiding the difficulties – domestic or intellectual – of composition: no apologies for that. As Stephen Vizinczey says in the remarkable *Truth and Lies in Literature*, to be a writer you need all the brains you've got.

Removing the economic subsidies to Canadian publishers, as Hoffer wants to, would be an act of cultural suicide. If they were removed, there would be no Canadian publishers. They simply could not compete with American publishers, who have massive tax and tariff protections Canadian publishers do not have, along with a protected market that is ten times the size of Canada's to sell into. Similar conditions prevail for a variety of cultural industries in this country, and no one in his right mind should object to the modest subsidies provided by the federal government and a few enlightened provincial and local governments. A large part of the reason this country still exists is directly related to the work of these subsidized organizations. No book publisher I know of in Canada is rolling in gravy. Hoffer, incidentally, argues against subsidies from a curiously vulnerable position on this matter. If he were more circumspect he would reveal the genetically-related benefactor who has allowed his own business to survive over the years.

Like many people, I have a number of quite specific ideas about how the activities and constitution of the Canada Council could and should be altered. But I do not think the organization should be disbanded, nor do I think that its funding should be cut. It has, over the years, done an excellent job of fostering and protecting Canadian culture. Part of the way it has accomplished this is by subsidizing valuable artists across the country, many of whom are presently (if temporarily) foot soldiers and officers in Hoffer's bizarre army of cultural apocalypse. Some of these writers might have ceased to write long ago without the subsidies, and almost all of them would have been unable to publish except maybe by becoming the exploitees of Hoffer's occasional letterpress books only wealthy print lovers can afford.

Like the Social Credit government in British Columbia and like the governments of those states that were theoretically defeated in World War II, Hoffer seems to believe that only the physically strong or cunning should survive. He ignores the fact that subsidization of artists has been a normal practice since the beginning of human civilization. Most of those subsidy systems have been considerably less efficient than the present one. We do not know how many Rilkes or Shakespeares have been lost to starvation (or chartered accountancy) across the last few centuries because they were not born rich, lacked social or political cunning, or failed to acquire wealthy patrons. Hoffer's proposals are simple-minded, brutal and ignorant. Does he actually believe that art is some sort of subtext of *Triumph of the Will*?

Where Hoffer and I did agree, and still do, is over the degree to which our governments' efforts to create a national literature and a national identity have resulted in an inward-looking and essentially amateur literature. Too many of the books published in this country (including some of my own earliest ones) are opportunistic and amateurish: they are published without any notion that a book should have a coherent relationship to its intended audience, and most of them are not composed as books at all – they are merely an emptying of an accumulated academic curriculum vitae. The majority of these amateur books are collections of trivial verse, and there are so many of them around that they have destroyed their readership.

Hoffer simplistically blames the Canada Council. I've argued, and will continue to, that aside from the misguided ambitions of the authors themselves, it is the university literature and creative writing departments that are to blame, and that the abuses inherent in the Canada Council, at least where writing and publishing are concerned, are a direct consequence of the administrative domination of the Council by polite folks from Rosedale, Westmount and Kerrisdale who can live with a heritage-type culture but don't want truly avant-garde and experimental activity in the arts, and by the university-based academics. Most people will be hard pressed to deny the overwhelming evidence that in general the universities have failed during the last two decades, both as institutes of public cultural education and as institutions of advanced learning.

There are two main reasons for this. The first is that the universities have mistaken the subject matter of literature. For publicly funded institutions, the subject matter of literature should be treated as cultural history and the history of ideas, not as the techniques by which academic readers are supposed to process literary works with a variety of arbitrary critical frameworks. Literature is first and finally about how the world works, not about the formal aesthetic techniques by which the writers work. The latter subject matter is for specialists, and even here the universities have failed: our university graduate programs in literature teach specialists how to become critics, and how to perpetuate the current hierarchy in which critics are at the top in both income and prestige and working artists are at the bottom.

The second reason why the universities failed has to do with simple demographics: the rapid expansion of universities in this country and elsewhere during the 1960s overloaded them with mediocre intellectuals more interested in job security, middle-class splendour and tenure-track privileges than in intellectual matters. Now, twenty years later, they are shadowing their jobs and defending their specialties against all comers, teaching courses they memorized a decade ago, and trying to keep the barbarians out of their Volvo-filled driveways. One of their chief specialties is CanLit. Exacerbating the problem is that many of them both teach and write CanLit.

Most of the CanLit specialists are quite nice people. Some of them are talented writers, and many might be better if they had the time and motivation to write. Mostly, however, they write short, 19th-century poems. They choose this form because writing this kind of closed aesthetic verse takes less time and commitment than any other writing medium. Most of what they write is self-consciously apolitical, which is to say, academic and trivial.

That the CanLit folks have grown to dominate the activities of the Canada Council isn't surprising, either. Most of them are careerists, and they have lots of experience with committee and inter-agency politics. That the Council is able to do as many interesting things as it does, under the circumstances, is what ought to surprise us.

Early on in our discussion, Hoffer and I began to differ sharply on two related questions: honesty and professionalism. I happen to believe that most people are basically honest and that literally everyone believes in their own sincerity. Consequently, it seemed to me that a frontal assault based on the issue of sincerity would be unsuccessful, leaving only failure or some form of increasingly unattractive intellectual violence as an alternative. If we were serious about improving our cultural and literary production, I argued, whatever private antagonisms we harboured would have to be jettisoned or laid on the table for scrutiny, and a less punitive approach taken. I therefore challenged Hoffer to articulate his position by providing a *written* statement of what he had in mind.

Hoffer weaseled on this point, and around the time that our quite natural antagonism toward one another began to obscure the real issues, I began to realize that Hoffer was harbouring a hidden agenda, one that even he was not aware of: his hatred of "unreal" writers had very little to do with either the Canada Council or the universities, and a great deal to do with his own inability or unwillingness to write. In short, his rage is the product of jealousy, albeit of a very unusual variety.

As a failed Marxist, Hoffer can still fantasize that the state will wither away, despite the fact that the revolution hasn't come in any form that an evangelical Marxist would recognize. For a fundamentalist like Hoffer, because neither the revolution nor the withering away of the state has occurred, life is impure. And he just can't bear impurity. More important, he refuses to write while impurities exist. Writing, to him, is "dishonourable," and since he can't bring himself to do it, he wants to stop everyone else from writing.

That's just plain crazy. Artists of all kinds work precisely because imperfect conditions exist. At the most simple level, that imperfection is the chief source of artistic energy. And anyone who reads the correspondence Hoffer published will understand my response to my discovery of Hoffer's private agenda. I made it clear in the workshops that I was interested only in seeing the writers get better, and that I was not interested in an encounter group. I'm not a psychiatrist, however much Hoffer appeared to want one.

Hoffer gave me his story and poems to read, I assumed, on a professional basis, and I edited them and gave them back to him. I do that for anyone who sends me a piece of writing in draft form. It's a courtesy, and I believe it is how writers should socialize, instead of merely mumbling the customary "far out" to one another in response to work offered for scrutiny. I see editing draft work as practice, much the same as the way baseball players play catch, or hit and field ground balls with one another. If writers don't discuss literature and culture and edit one another's work, all they'll do is sit around complaining about how nobody pays enough attention to them, and how much they dislike everyone who doesn't happen to be in the room. I don't enjoy that.

Hoffer has subsequently produced a small number of extremely expensive chapbooks by the few authors in Canada willing to talk to him. This is, one supposes, his alternative program to what now passes as Canadian publishing. It's interesting to note that originally his program of cultural Armageddon was far more ambitious. After the Final Judgement Construction Co. came its military equivalent, with the grandiose title of *Tanks Are Mighty Fine Things*. It was supposed to involve a magazine that displayed the values and talents of his chosen literary superpersons. Being an optimist, I figured that the journal wouldn't go beyond a single issue, knowing that continuity and consistency aren't Hoffer's long suits at the best of times. He likes to make grand gestures, and he wanted the magazine and the publishing program to make a grand statement he'd be able to whack his imagined enemies about the head and shoulders with. And of course, he plans to make some money selling off the balance of the small print runs of the books at inflated prices to the universities. He's a bookseller, remember. As he himself points out in his preface to the published correspondence, he's been making his living off the specialty book trade and the universities for sixteen years. That's something I can't claim, and wouldn't want to.

Meanwhile, the discourse over the role of the universities and the Canada Council in producing the cultural amateurism that dogs Canadian writing desperately needs to take place. Globalist cultural and economic pressures are likely to force a general debate on the value of national culture upon the academic and writing communities in the next decade anyway. I think, as a beginning, we should recognize that government subsidies are not the primary issue. The distribution of subsidies is an important issue, but one that will be resolved in the context of this larger discussion, probably in ways no one is going to like much.

I'm an economic and cultural nationalist in the sense that I believe that Canada must remain – or is it "become"? – distinct and independent, both in its economy and its cultural institutions. Cultural protection and economic subsidies for the publishing industry are two legitimate and essential methods of achieving that. One of the things that keeps Canadian writers from being more effective than they are and from achieving international status and audience is that they keep slipping on, and into, the watery gravy that leaks from the universities. A harrowing of the universities, and the academic habits and values they take for granted, is the first step toward a better literature and a truly viable national culture.

Privately published and circulated

POLITICS AND THE ENGLISH LANGUAGE (1991)

Almost a half century has passed since George Orwell wrote "Politics and the English Language". For most English-speaking writers who have had a strong desire to discover and tell the truth, the essay has been a basic text. In it, Orwell argued that clear thinking and good writing are integral to the health of democracy, and that bad language can and does corrupt thought. Those ideas are almost self-evident truths today, and the detailed arguments Orwell made in the essay remain remarkably current. My renovation of the essay's contents will therefore be – as my title suggests – a bracketed and respectful addendum.

Since 1946, when Orwell published his essay, there have been profound changes in the way human beings speak, write, and use knowledge. Radio, television and a number of less public but powerful cybernetic technologies now occupy our days, often filling our heads with information we either haven't asked for or don't have the right equipment or the wealth to make use of. We "communicate" or "process information" through immensely powerful and fast electronic systems, but we write less, and, I suspect, think less. Certainly the critical thought going on these days concerning the crucial subjects of politics and culture is in a state of conceptual disarray. Contemporary electronic communications are a matter of fewer and fewer people speaking to (and for) more and more people.

Despite this, the English language itself has taken only one major turn Orwell didn't foresee. In 1946, he feared that the undefeated totalitarianisms of World War II would breed Newspeak, the official language of his novel *1984*. Newspeak made understanding impossible by truncating or outlawing all the textures and nuances of language. But instead of Newspeak, the 1990s are filled with techno-gibberish dialects that glamourize the obvious and the trivial, and obscure (or sever) connections to other fields of meaning. The intent of these dialects is to make it difficult for anyone to communicate beyond their "lifestyle" enclave. The dialects serve the same purpose as Newspeak – creating political silence – by conning us into thinking that we're somehow more fashionable and smarter than the next enclave, and by getting us to fiddle endlessly with an assortment of disposable commodities, fake threats to our well-being, and obsessive notions of correct behaviour that border on fanaticism.

What that means is that politics – or maybe it is just authority – has changed. Some changes have been for the better, and some haven't. Within the industrialized nations, violent authority can no longer successfully operate indefinitely, and police states have demonstrated that they simply aren't efficient enough to compete with cybernetic economies – as witnessed by the recent economic and political collapse of the Soviet bloc. Violent authority is still the rule outside the industrialized part of the world, where, if anything, life has become more violent and arbitrary. In the privileged societies like ours, authority has merely gotten itself out of our faces and into our lowest appetites. Universal social justice, it should be noted, is as distant as it has ever been.

For an individual trying to think and write accurately in the intellectual and informational environments of the 1990s, politics are no longer a matter of complaining about the stupidity or corruption of the government. Politics – and they are a plural now – are the things we do to one another, or allow to be done to us by others through indifference or lust or whatever we've decided is self-interest. As the millennium nears, and as the referent ideologies that have guided and/or deluded us through the century collapse around us, politics have more to do with how we allow ourselves to be lied to and deceived than how we are imprisoned or liberated. In the industrialized democracies, most of us are free as the birds. We just happen to be turkeys and chickens, with a few aggressive but deluded raptors tossed into the mix to make the peaceful cower and to give the brainlessly ambitious something to aspire to.

Communists, capitalists, fascists and all the permutations in between have become meaningless epithets. Orwell himself saw that coming. Everything he wrote from *Homage to Catalonia* to his death argues against the structuring of politics by ideological claim. For us, his essay "Second Thoughts on James Burnham" (1946) ought to be read as the companion piece to "Politics and the English Language" because it reveals his characteristic skill at eluding the seductive ideological nets of his time. In that essay he summarizes Burnham's future scenario in *The Managerial Revolution* (1940) in terms that will be chillingly familiar to us: "Capitalism is disappearing, but socialism is not replacing it. What is now arising is a new kind of planned, centralized society which will be neither capitalist nor, in any accepted sense of the word, democratic. The rulers of this new society will be the people who effectively control the means of production: that is, business executives, technicians, bureaucrats and soldiers, lumped together by Burnham under the name of 'managers'." That's a fair description of the corporate oligarchy that controls the world today – an oligarchy that operates on eighteen-month financial horizons and proudly promises an end to the excesses of ideological politics. That Orwell was able to foresee and critique the weaknesses of a vast political change that contemporary analysts are just now learning to bend their minds around is typical of just how brilliant his intellectual method was.

Understanding how the new politics work will require a few conceptual simplifications. One of them is recognizing that there are only three kinds of political beings in the world. First, there are people who will try to see and tell the truth, and try to act on it in the interests of everyone. Second, there are – let me put this as succinctly as possible – assholes. Third, there are people who are too weakened by poverty, disease and violence to care about being either of the first two. Good politics consists of behaviours that enlarge the numbers of type A and reduce, without violence or arrogance, the numbers of types B and C. I'm pretty sure that George Orwell would agree with this simplification.

In the new environment, clear political writing and thinking is perhaps more urgently needed than ever. It remains an essential component of democracy – which is, after all, not a political state but a social, intellectual and moral activity. For that activity to regain the alertness it requires to be effective, the toolbox a political writer needs to deal with the 1990s needs some additions.

I'm going to suggest a few tools. For the sake of convenience, I'll divide them into two categories, practical and conceptual. Most of the practical ones have to do with keeping writing direct and simple and personal, which is the only antidote I know for the poison of technogibberish. The conceptual tools I use are generally attitudinal tactics aimed at inducing and nourishing the habitual skepticism Orwell taught me. What follows isn't meant to be either an exclusive or exhaustive toolbox on its own, merely an addition to Orwell's. Intellectual tools don't work the same way for everyone, but I can at least testify that the ones I offer help me to keep my eyes open in the cyclone of lies daily life has become. And sometimes, they help me to close them with laughter.

PRACTICAL WRITING TOOLS

1. George Orwell's "Politics and the English Language" ought to be reread about every six months. Nearly everything he said remains relevant. His examples should be periodically updated with your own.

2. Write simple sentences whenever you can, and let your musicianship take care of the need for melody. If you've got a tin ear, get into another line of work.

3. Fill your writing with nouns and verbs. Naming things accurately makes them palpable, and making them move in specific ways enables them to be tested. Beware of adjectives and adverbs because they are linguistic grease. Using more than two successive adjectives in a single sentence is a reliable signal that a Mazola party is going on in the writer's head.

4. Never use a semicolon. I know I'm repeating Orwell, but this is so important it bears repeating. Semicolons are absolutely reliable signals that a sentence should be rewritten, generally to make it more direct. And incidentally, you should only use a colon if you're wearing a tuxedo or sitting on white porcelain.

5. Contemporary writers should learn how to use a word processor, and how to manipulate data systems. If you're a working writer, it is more important to own a word processor than a car. Word processors are necessary to keep up to the current speeds of information transmission and production, and because having other people decipher your lousy hand-writing is vile and exploitive political behaviour.

CONCEPTUAL TOOLS

1. Beware of sacred cattle. They are stupid, filled with inflated ideas about their importance and the unimportance of everything in their projected path, and if you let them run around inside your head they will eat or trample everything, including your intelligence. On the other hand, do not attempt to run anyone else's sacred cattle over a

cliff unless you're certain you can succeed. Today's sacred cattle are a new and much more dangerous breed than the ones that emerged in the 1950s and are now dying out. The new breed are very aggressive, they're used to living in information-overloaded cities, and if you wave a red flag at them they'll pin you to the nearest concrete abutment without a qualm.

2. Good political writing always recognizes when it is running in a stampede and attempts to get out of it as quickly as possible, preferably without trying to work the herd. This is a fancy way of saying that the job of a political writer is to ask the questions that aren't being addressed by the visible agendas of authority or exclusive interest. Generally speaking, figuring out – or making up – answers is someone else's job – someone you probably won't trust or like. Never trust anyone with an answer to a question you haven't asked.

3. Recognize that everyone is sincere and that sincerity has no relationship to anything but righteousness, which is an enemy of good political writing, and usually, death to clear thinking. Accusing anyone of insincerity precludes the possibility of further political debate, and you're supposed to be writing in order to start and keep people talking to one another.

4. The language of political speeches and official communiques is never meaningless. Most of the time, speeches, press releases and official communiques are cybernetic devices meant to occupy a vital political moment or space without committing the originating speaker, institution or agency to action. They require full translation, which involves an analysis of what they both say and don't say. This is also true of commercial language, which is becoming indistinguishable from political language.

5. If you don't believe in God, don't quote Her. By this I mean that writers must try to be personal, and should not make their voices out to be more than they are – the words and gestures of a single person who has thought through and researched a subject matter. Practising this successfully involves a number of mental habits, some of which are as follows:

a) never using the word "we" unless you know who you're collectivizing and are willing to kiss them all on the mouth – and mean it.

b) never using the word "reality" without putting quotes around it.

c) recognizing that there is no such thing as a rhetorical question.

d) never dismissing a dead or older writer for not knowing what is currently fashionable around the office or inside your dopey head.

e) remembering that the surface of any important truth will more resemble the skin of a toad than an alabaster statue or brochure materials that promise to make you into a human bullet. Warts are not something that will disappear from writing and thinking just because we don't approve of bumps and lesions. They're what used to be called texture, and without texture there is no such thing as meaning. Bullets, whatever form they come in, are the opposite of meaning, and they are signals of the collapse of human intelligence.

6. Try not to contribute to the cacaphony of disinformation and nonsense. In a democracy the only opinion anyone is entitled to is an informed and preferably detailed one. If all you're hearing is the sound of your own voice, silence is the right option.

7. Finally, make people laugh with your writing. Laughter disrupts narrow logic, which is the operating system for authority, cattle stampedes, and ill-conceived judgments of all sorts. People who are laughing find it hard to start wars, molest children, and are unlikely to discover that the person or persons in their immediate vicinity are in league with the devil. Orthodoxy most easily breeds where laughter is absent.

Written at the request of Canadian University Press and presumably published in their 1991 Handbook

Part 2:
FOR
CIVIL
INTERVENTIONS

UNUSUAL CIRCUMSTANCES

Not too long ago, somewhere in Ontario, a man was hit by lightning under very unusual circumstances.

"Bad thinking and writing," I can hear you say. "Isn't getting hit by lightning already an unusual circumstance? Isn't it, in fact, the standard illustration of how totally unpredictable life is?"

Yes, indeed. But remember, I said that the circumstances were *very* unusual. Anyone can get hit by lightning. I'm talking about someone who got zapped in a very special and educative way.

There were two oddities about this lightning strike that qualify it as a *very* unusual circumstance. The first was that the victim had a neurotic fear of lightning. He'd sought out just the kind of job he thought would offer him the maximum possible protection from what he feared. That created the second oddity. He was 6000 feet underground when he was struck by the lightning.

I'm not making this up. The victim was working inside a mine, repairing the steel cage that carries the miners from the surface to the ore deposit. The lightning bolt hit the elevator cable housing at the mine surface and travelled down. Snap, Crackle, Pop.

Don't be alarmed. I'm not suggesting that we're in any immediate danger, despite the 100 percent probability of a major earthquake somewhere near us before the year 2000, the spilled viruses down at the recently reopened biological warfare labs *(For God's sake hold that beaker upright, Igor!)* that may wipe out our species any day now, or that out-of-control Ford bearing down on one of your loved ones as you read this. I'll quite cheerfully admit that when lightning hits someone, it's bad luck. Beyond that, I think there are rational limits on how much precaution people should take against an unsafe world. If we're rich we can rebuild our houses so they won't fall down when the earthquakes hit. I'm not sure what we can do about Igor except to elect governments that don't spend their energies devising ways to kill people. The auto industry is building safer cars, but the traffic deaths don't seem to be any fewer.

Good, rational people with social democratic values don't, of course, believe in luck, and they try not to think about things like getting hit by lightning because it suggests that the world can't be made safe. Yet despite rationality, people keep getting hit by lightning, and the safety nets we build don't always work. Our friend 6000 feet beneath the surface went to absurd lengths – or depths – to avoid a lightning strike and it got him anyway. He probably suffered unimaginable terrors before the event, and almost certainly he had a terrible life because of his fears. Mines aren't pleasant work-places, and the basements and underground malls he must have preferred outside working hours don't conjure up quality-of-life images.

So while I'm not quite suggesting that the dangers you and I face are immediate and unavoidable, I definitely do mean to suggest that we may be paying too high a price for our personal safety. I mean, while we're going through the necessary struggles to create error-free technologies, safe food and drugs, and equitable procedures for compensating injured workers and all that, maybe we're losing sight of other, even more important things.

I probably should explain what I mean by "we". I'm a committed (if irritable and occasionally irresponsible) social democrat. That means I get accused by my family of being a communist – a term that a few years ago meant "devil" but these days merely means that they think I'm a financial nitwit. My enemies, because I come from the north and don't like being supervised, occasionally decide that I'm a right-wing anarchist or worse. Whatever I really am, it is my personal belief that social democrats and other liberal-minded people are *supposed* to be projecting a world based on the positive values of social democracy, philosophical liberalism and equitable social, economic and political justice. But we're not doing that these days. We seem to be spending most of our energies demanding industrial and personal safety from the commodities and the technology we're surrounded by.

Having a safe world is part of social democracy, but it sure as hell isn't the whole program. Just a decade or two back, we wanted quite a lot more. Back then we were demanding a just world, one in which services and opportunities would be distributed equally, by elected governments who we thought would soon be proudly social democratic or even socialist. But somehow, we've been red-scared and consumerized into political oblivion, outslicked, and just plain outsmarted. Recent international events now make it seem like we got sideswiped by history itself, at least if you believe those philosophers down at *Time* and *Maclean's* who are crowing about the triumph of capitalism.

Because of all these drubbings we've changed into something less than we were. Repeated defeat doesn't seem to have strengthened our resolve or made us wiser. It has given us a fundamentally different, and diminished, operating logic, one that is somehow less generous and tolerant than it ought to be.

So you're clear about what I'm accusing us of, here's what I see as the current political strategy of the left:

If we can't control the political and social character of our society, we can at least ensure, by our lobbies or simply by righteous interpersonal bullying, that it be safe for cautious, ordinary citizens, their children, and god damnit to hell, all those irresponsible people who aren't interested in being safe.

Our economic strategy is similar, except that it's even more myopic and small-minded:

If we can't or don't want to alter or challenge the capitalist economic system we live under, we can at least insist that it be safe for workers, that an accurate gender and racial ratio be ground up in its gears, and that adequate compensation be paid to the victims.

There's nothing intrinsically wrong with these strategies except that they make social democrats sound like actuarial experts or marketing personnel for the bicycle helmet manufacturing industry. They're not wrong, but they're kind of, well, chickenshit. I don't know about you, but I became a social democrat because I believe that people ought to be treated with decency and kindness, not because I want them to be hemmed in by safety devices so they don't harm themselves. Capitalism isn't kind or decent, and neither was communism or socialism, which were all too willing to impose crude and cruel dictatorships of one sort or another on behalf of abstract principles. Islamic fundamentalism enjoys making women wear uncomfortable clothing and cutting off sinners' hands far too much to suit me, and Christian fundamentalism doesn't offer any vision of decency or kindness at all. It's just a bunch of white guys with Cadillacs committing indecent acts while their organizations try to screw the young, the gullible and the elderly financially. Social democracy is and remains the one political instrument we have to express our kindly and humane impulses.

But social democracy seems to have lost more than its sense of perspective. It has also lost its sense of fun. We've become the rancorous hostages of our own retreat and reaction to an era in which the once immanent coming-to-political-power of social democracy has been supervened and swept aside by such moral marvels as Ronald Reagan and Margaret Thatcher. Neoconservativism has managed, in a few short years, to replace the principles and values of social justice with the deification of opportunity, and it has supplanted humanism with a Dictatorship of the Entrepreneurs.

A few years ago American humourist P.J. O'Rourke coined the phrase "Safety Nazi" to describe the behavioural residue of the liberal left's collapse. Safety Nazis, he explained, are those people who harbour an unreasoning hatred for anything observably or statistically unhealthy and/or unsafe. For instance, their loathing for cigarette smokers has become so virulent that they're prepared to make life a living (or at least outdoor) hell for smokers, and occasionally they're even prepared to attack them physically in public places. They're also responsible for those safety lids on consumer products that take a three-week training course to open. Fair enough, you might want to argue, but remember that these people want safety lids on any substance you'd have to ingest ten gallons of in a two-hour period before it gave you even a mild headache, let alone cancer.

They're the same folks who are in favour of sensible shoes, mandatory automotive airbags, squash pie enemas and enforced aerobic exercise. They're against synthetic fabrics, highly processed foods, perfume, scotch whisky, practical jokes, irreverence and silliness – and they'll kick your face off if you disagree with them.

They're the ones who equip their cars with those motion-sensitive alarm systems that are always waking us up in the middle of the night, and they're prone to strap all valuable objects – including children – to the walls in case of earthquake, criminals or an outbreak of simple human stupidity. Among their recent victories was the banning of lawn darts – a stunning accomplishment in a world that sees governments spending a trillion dollars annually on lethal military weapons.

O'Rourke was mostly concerned that in wiping out risk we're killing all the fun in life. I take fun, and the term "Safety Nazi", a little more seriously. We're living in a society in which the "progressive" elements are spending far more of their energies worrying over short-term private safety measures – enforced wearing of automotive safety belts or stamping out those responsible for sidestream chromium pollution – than the threat of a nuclear holocaust or bio-tech collapse or good old-fashioned mass injustice and oppression.

A couple of years ago, for instance, the annual conference of an organization of Canadian writers – writers are supposed to be our unacknowledged legislators and antennae, if you recall – degenerated into a virtual donnybrook over whether delegates were allowed to smoke cigarettes during plenary sessions and workshops. Not only did the argument obliterate discussion throughout the meetings on the plethora of crucial issues facing writers, but the debate raged on for at least six months in the pages of the organization's newsletter. Friendships ended and radical smoking and anti-smoking factions formed, and the general hostility about the issue has clouded meetings on more than one occasion since, even though the non-smokers have more or less won the fight. And who hasn't heard a once-sane social democrat make a remark like "Well I agree with so-and-so's stance on the Palestinians or Free Trade, but you know, he's a smoker, and I just can't bear to be in the same room with him"?

Please don't mistake what I'm saying. Safety Nazis are well-intentioned, virtuous people. Most of the time they're right about what they're insisting on. We should wear safety belts and we should give up our cars for bicycles and those ginky-looking plastic helmets. We should all stop smoking cigarettes, and considerate smokers certainly shouldn't insist on polluting the homes of non-smokers.

I know I should wear a seat belt when I drive, but more often than not, I don't. I also happen to smoke cigarettes, and I'm thoroughly aware that it is killing me. For sure, it is reducing my range of social opportunities and narrowing my circle of friends. I've learned to buckle up when one of my kids insists – and whenever I see a cop. I also intend to quit smoking soon. But just to be mischievous I tell non-smoking assailants that I intend to die in an oxygen tent explosion – hopefully about forty years from now – trying to light just one last cigarette. It's my way of insisting that there are more important threats to life and limb than deleterious personal or consumer habits.

Whenever I happen to find myself arguing with one of these

small-minded Safety Nazis, I catch myself thinking about something former Yale University Chaplain Sloan Coffin once said. It was during the 1970s, and I think he was talking about the U.S. Congress during the Nixon Administration, but what he said fits the liberal left during the late 1980s and early 1990s even better. It was not, as the Bible has it, that there were not ten righteous men in Sodom, he said. There were no doubt ten, forty, four hundred, maybe even four thousand righteous men, and there were probably quite a few more righteous women. The problem was that *their righteousness just wasn't relevant.*

What I'm suggesting is quite simple. Those of us who support the basic values of social democracy ought to be doing more than merely complaining about what assholes our fellow consumers are, and browbeating those we decide aren't behaving correctly or safely. We need to stop mistaking consumer virtue for political reality. Life just isn't entirely safe, and insisting that it should be – to the current point of lunacy – is draining our political energies. We've got to return to our original visions of a just and equitable world, and stop this rancorous bickering with one another while we still have some rights to work with other than the right to consume. This is too unusual a circumstance to be caught fighting among ourselves when the lightning strikes.

This Magazine

ELUDING THE STAMPEDE

Over the past several years, both its members and outsiders have criticized the Writers Union of Canada and the Canadian publishing industry for being male dominated, and, well, too WASP. The criticisms are sincere and they're frequently passionate, but as writers are supposed to know better than most people, sincerity and passion are hardly guarantees to either accuracy or relevance.

Debate at 1988's annual general meeting of the Writers Union, for instance, was complicated by a chronically outraged and enraged writer named Sheila Conway, who attempted to feminize then-chairperson Pierre Berton's pronouns every time he used one. If that had been all she did, no one would have much cared. Berton still lives on Planet of the Guys, and pronoun parity has become a technical reality only among writers under 50. But Conway took things further, accusing Berton and the Union along with him of everything from gender-parity heresy to fascist machismo. Her criticism didn't have much impact, because while Planet of the Guys is still in orbit inside Pierre Berton's head and around most of society, it isn't within the Union. The incoming chairperson was Betty Jane Wylie, and the majority of the Union's most articulate and influential members are women – people like Susan Crean, June Callwood, Merrily Weisbord, Heather Menzies, Libby Scheier and Myrna Kostash.

Conway's warlock-hunt, however, accidentally generated a much more accurate criticism of the Union, this one concerning the scarcity of visible cultural and racial minorities within its ranks. And indeed, the Union's membership *is* overwhelmingly white and middle-class. When the issue was raised at one of the plenary sessions, one had only to look around the room to confirm that it was true.

The problem was that no one quite knew what to do about it. Some sensible suggestions were made that a conscious effort to recruit minority writers should be undertaken – a difficult task given the Union's eligibility criteria – and everyone left the session feeling vaguely uneasy about it. Notwithstanding that the "dominant" Anglophone demographic in Canada only produces about 20 percent of the books sold in this country (the rest come overwhelmingly from the U.S.), it *is* true that our visible minorities – Native Indians, and our growing Caribbean and Asian populations – have at best a marginal publishing voice. They have their own presses, but they're not very good and the distribution they get is abysmal. The federal government's various and largely cynical multiculturalism programs have made the problem harder to deal with. About all they accomplish is to saddle WASPS – and everyone else – with a veritable deluge of new sacred cattle. Because these new sacred cattle are the inviolable intellectual property of their creators, no one knows exactly why they're sacred, or where and when they're permitted to be confronted or restrained like our now seedy and docile WASP sacred cattle have been. We're clear about two things: WASPS are not allowed to annoy the new sacred cattle, and they're not allowed to ignore them. Doing either is racism.

Over the winter, the uneasiness over racism underwent a number of mutations, and it emerged on the 1989 AGM agenda in several different forms. The craziest one involved a controversy that started in Toronto's Women's Press, which defenestrated a couple of writers from an anthology for something called structural racism. In the absence of minority writers to speak for their constituencies, the braintrust at the Women's Press reasoned, WASP writers should desist from writing about the culturally disadvantaged and the racially different – and, apparently, cease even to imagine their condition.

It wasn't clear to anyone precisely what this cease-and-desist order meant, or who it applied to. It was pretty clear that it covered WASPs, particularly male WASPs. But did it mean that white ethnics – the semi-visible minorities – could no longer write about visible minorities? Could, say, a black feminist writer write about Asians? Could Caribbean blacks write about American or African blacks? Could minority writers write about WASPs? Could gay women write about heterosexual women? Could gay males write about women, were transsexuals to write about their destination or their departure gender, and what gender subject matters were correct for transvestites? Did it mean that WASPs were to cease to even imagine the conditions of non-WASPs, and if so, wasn't this prohibiting them from trying to do precisely what they're being censured for being incapable of?

The issue dominated the Union's confidential "Inner Circle" section of the newsletter all winter. One side coalesced around the position that writers creating characters from the visible minorities or from economically disadvantaged classes are guilty of exploiting them, and should forthwith exercise self-censorship, i.e. shut the fuck up. The other side took the classic civil libertarian stance, arguing that any form of censorship is unacceptable, and that the acceptance of the Women's Press position would result in a situation where writers would be able to write only about themselves. Such a circumstance might be okay for the League of Canadian Poets, but not for the Union, which is made up mostly of fiction and non-fiction writers for whom an inverted sensorium in which gazing at sunsets or worrying over how they feel about their ancestors is reasonably foreign. For sure, the spectre of still more white middle-class and middle-aged writers unable to write about anything except how they experience their inner selves within a reference base circumscribed by New Age WASP preoccupations is a truly frightening one.

The racism issue landed in everyone's laps on the 1989 AGM's first morning with a panel discussion of racism in publishing. June Callwood presided over a panel that consisted of Lenore Keeshig-Tobias, a Native story-teller, Dr. Moiz Vassanji, editor of the *Toronto South Asian Review*, and M&S publisher Doug Gibson. Keeshig-Tobias, who has clearly spent more time at professional guilt conferences mind-fucking white folks than she has doing scholarly research into the origins and universality of myths, browbeat the audience with admirable self-assurance and some very real skill. Eventually she warned us, with a delicious lack of irony, that a "Committee to Reestablish the Trickster" was in the process of developing the means to replace Western middle-class artistic procedures and institutions with tricks more appropriate to a First Nation.

Vassanji, by contrast, was sensible and modest, pointing out that yes indeed, there is racism in Canadian culture and publishing, and that yes, there is also a globalized and homogenizing marketplace out there which almost no one *in any sector of the culture is really able to resist effectively*. When Gibson got up and declared that there was *no* racism in Canadian publishing, it was clear he was taking for granted a totally different universe from the one Keeshig-Tobias was taking for granted. The result was a pudding of intellectual non sequiturs, albeit sincerely tossed in from all sides.

The fog refused to clear as the AGM progressed – or rather, digressed. No one really believes that there is deliberate racism within the Union membership, and the conceptual conundrum of structural racism was one that no one wanted to debate, not in the absence of an accepted taxonomy to sort out the sacred cattle. No one wanted to see a stampede, either, and consequently there was a multiplicity of soothing cattle-calls being quietly murmured, and the few genuine cattle-prods in the room were being brandished with extreme politeness. The result wasn't a debate at all, but a confused choir of disinterested or cautious mooos and a lot of milling around in the meadow. Then, late in the proceedings, a resolution to establish a task force on racism landed on the floor.

This initiative was greeted with an enthusiasm that can only be described as, well, *wan*. When someone asked what the task force ought to do, there was silence. Some members said they thought it ought to study racism in publishing. Studying someone else's problem would have been a safe enough dodge, but no one really wanted to dodge the issue. Yet the room was so filled with sacred cattle that no one could quite see how to approach it. Any substantive declaration of intentions involved the risk of stepping on sensitive toes – or hooves. Nearly everyone in the room felt that the proposed resolution contained nothing more than good intentions, but no one was going to stand up and say so for fear of being accused of being indifferent to racism. The resolution's backers weren't making it clear what they had in mind for the task force, or why it deserved the extreme measure of an emergency task force. It wasn't until one of the AGM's few minority writers asked them to clarify these questions that anyone understood that the people behind the resolution had no idea what they were doing. There was an audible sigh of relief when the resolution was defeated – or, more precisely, sent back to its instigators for more, uh, conceptual development.

While all this was going on with all the seriousness and tension of the United Nations debating the spread of biological weapons, a small group of writers who hadn't completely lost their sense of humour convened in one of the lounges to create a practical vehicle that would satisfy the demands of the self-censorship crowd. The tongue-in-cheek solution they came up with – in about 25 minutes – was that writers ought to create a character bank. Each writer would detail a character based on him- or herself and place it into the bank vault, so that writers in search of narratives that went beyond mere monologue could withdraw, for a fee, properly authenticated, licenced characters.

The character bank seemed like a thoroughly rational solution for about another ten minutes, when someone realized that withdrawn characters would have to be politically correct. That would mean that they'd have the right to express correct attitudes and opinions at all times, along with the power to veto their behaviour in the stories they participated in. Moreover, no characters could be placed in life-threatening situations without being equipped with the appropriate safety devices – safety straps, crash helmets, Kevlar vests, prophylactics, mouth dams, etc. In order to protect their dignity as characters, no insults or jokes could be made, and all sides to arguments would have to be presented.

A few of the writers were willing to proceed with the character bank anyway, until someone pointed out that the characters would quickly form a Characters Union of Canada, and demand to have their own AGM, and who the hell would pay for that? In the end, like everything else at the Writers Union AGM, the character bank was shelved for further conceptual development. Meanwhile, what never got asked was the basic question. Is racism a problem in Canadian writing and publishing?

There are racist writers in Canada, certainly, and they can be found both in and outside the WASP majority. The WASP racists tend to stay in the closet these days – and they seem to steer well clear of the Writers Union. Almost as certainly, writers from minorities have more difficulty getting books into mainstream print than WASP writers do, mostly because market economies of scale make it a financial absurdity to publish books for audiences that aren't large enough to make publishing remotely profitable. Publishing minority writers' books simply because they represent minority views might be a demonstration of the political correctness and wide coverage of federal multicultural programs, but it isn't likely to be of much interest or utility to anyone else, including, ultimately, the minorities. Poor sales and distribution will simply be a confirmation of economic marginality, and it might push minorities further into isolation from the mainstream.

The Women's Press call for self-censorship is probably well-intentioned enough, despite the Trotskyite appearances. Seen in the best possible light, the call seems aimed at stopping careless writers from depicting people in their writing without bothering to find out how those people see themselves. The controversy already generated will probably make a lot of writers think twice about writing up elements of this culture they don't have any experience of. But despite the good intentions, the consequences of uncritically accepting self-censorship have a dark side. If writers voluntarily give up imagining the consciousness of those who are culturally and psychologically unlike themselves, the gulf between those on whom this society confers advantages and those it oppresses or ignores is going to widen.

The theoretical purpose of a democracy is to create multiplicity and differentiation – to encourage, within the context of the rule of law, as many different, independent human beings as there are citizens. In this respect, democratic values are more important than those of multiculturalism. If women, including women of colour, are being subjected to violence, or are not being accorded equal treatment before the law, then that involves an abrogation of democratic rights, and the situation must be corrected in accordance with the rule of law. It's quite a different kind of offence if someone is unhappy because someone else is imagining or writing about them in ways that don't depict them as they see themselves.

Democracy is supposed to enable the individual pursuit of happiness, but it is not there to guarantee or enforce happiness. Only communism has tried to do that, and most of us now understand how little success it achieved, and what brutal degradations of the human spirit it perpetrated by its efforts. Notwithstanding any of this, Canadian minorities, particularly minority women, are still not being guaranteed the same riches of opportunity accorded to WASPs, and that is a serious inequity.

In the absence of simple solutions, we should probably be thinking about what the marketplace does to cattle, sacred or otherwise. With the advance of the Free Trade Agreement, the ascendancy of the International Monetary Fund as our planetary government, and other items in the neoconservatist agenda, mainstream Canadians and their writers are about to become a voiceless cultural minority like all the others. When that happens, maybe the issues will be clearer, and we will all find it easier to understand the differences between offending sacred cattle and protecting our rights.

Books in Canada

PIECES OF MEAT

The Wayne Gretzky Trade
as a Preview of Life
in the Free Trade Era

I had two quite unusual reactions when Wayne Gretzky was traded to the Los Angeles Kings. The first one lasted for about three or four hours after I heard on the radio that the Great One had been sold to Bruce McNall for $15 million. I was genuinely upset. Couldn't believe my ears. Went around the house mumbling about the obscene and violent acts I planned to commit upon the person of Peter Pocklington, the flat earth, summary execution and pork sausage advocate who owns the Edmonton Oilers. My second reaction, still stranger, came the next morning. I consulted the *Globe and Mail* to see what it had to say about the trade.

Getting upset about a hockey trade, however important, is a pretty odd thing for me. I don't like hockey, so I shouldn't have cared one way or another. It's a horrible, violent game, and children shouldn't be allowed to play it. I'm also less than fond of the *Globe and Mail*, which has become the chief source of reactionary, ill-considered opinion on every subject imaginable. Maybe it always was, but now it's on every second streetcorner in the country claiming that it's our national newspaper. Even its sports page seems to have grown reactionary, and I haven't read what it has to tell Canada about the Leafs, Argos and Jays without suspicion since its best writer, Allen Abel, quit and went off to write about China and other exotic fields of sport. Yet 24 hours after the Gretzky trade, I had the odd instinct that the *Globe and Mail* would reveal the dimensions of the trade more accurately than anyone.

Notwithstanding – to use a favoured technical term from the Free Trade Agreement that most Canadians are just now beginning to understand really means "although we said we wouldn't screw you" – those two quirky reactions, I have a fairly normal view of Canadian life. Like most people, I thought of Wayne Gretzky as a national treasure. If hockey were generally played the way he plays it, it would be a fine sport – or at least better than WWF wrestling. Unlike nearly everyone else in hockey, Gretzky is indisputably a nice person. He's polite, generously community-minded, married to an attractive American woman with blonde hair and buck teeth – I could go on praising him until we're all nauseous. I wouldn't go so far as to say I'd like my sons to grow up and be like him, but really, he's quite okay given the competition.

Gretzky's had a difficult life in some ways that few of us think about. He's been the personal property of, first, Nelson Skalbania and then Peter Pocklington, Bobbsey Twins of western Canadian real estate. Now he belongs to a coin collector in Los Angeles. Certainly he's had to face professional realities no cultural worker does. Imagine, for instance, Conrad Black over at *Saturday Night* offering $15 million, David Frum, and three future Governor General's Award nominees to *This Magazine* for Rick Salutin. Get what I mean?

The morning after The Trade, the *Globe and Mail* had an item about it on the front page, two on the editorial page and three in the sports section. A large-print editorial announced that The Trade was entirely Gretzky's idea, and assured us all that "Mr. Pocklington, who could probably have come up with a dozen sound business reasons for hanging on to his superstar, yielded gracefully." Columnist Jeffrey Simpson, whose job it is to provide editorial balance, *Globe and Mail*-style – which means that his ideas are even further to the right than the editorials but are written with better prose – appeared to blame the entire trade on Janet Jones, Gretzky's wife.

Certain that this had provided me with most of the ideological non-facts, I turned to sports columnist Al Strachan. Eschewing editorial page procedure, Strachan had done some research. He revealed that a trade had apparently been in the wind for some time, and that it had been initiated by Gretzky's former owner, Nelson Skalbania. Fronting for Jimmy Pattison, Skalbania had offered $22 million to reacquire his property for the Vancouver Canucks. Canucks owner Frank Griffiths subsequently queered the deal, seeing that it would probably mean a takeover of the team by Pattison, who, in Gretzky, would have owned the only really attractive and valuable asset the club has ever had. It must have been a nervous moment for Griffiths, since Pattison has managed to take over nearly every other business in B.C. that caught his fancy during the last twenty years. He was even offered the B.C. government at one point, but passed on it for reasons obvious to everyone but Bill Vander Zalm.

Unfortunately, the Skalbania initiative activated Pocklington's reptilian core. He woke up to the fact that Gretzky was worth an immense sum of money in 1988, but that four years later when his contract expired, he might be worth nothing – a free agent, able to walk away to the team of his choice, or to retirement. So Pocklington put Gretzky up for bids.

Enter Bruce McNall, new owner of the Los Angeles Kings. He had the money, undisputed control of his club, and a market that is just drooling for a sports hero with Gretzky's Archie Andrews personality. He offered Pocklington $15 million and four first round draft choices in return for Gretzky and a couple of bodyguards. Oiler GM Glen Sather, who'd been out fishing while the negotiations were going on, showed up in time to squeeze L.A.'s budding star Jimmy Carson out of McNall.

Strachan correctly insisted that Gretzky hadn't wanted the trade. Gretzky's fondness for Edmonton, where his civic stature is slightly above that of God, is well-known. He also likes Oiler GM Sather, his team-mates, and the high-speed European style of hockey the Oilers play. This, according to Strachan, was why Gretzky broke down at the press conference announcing the trade. Still, Gretzky reluctantly agreed to the trade, he said, because he's a "realist", and therefore recognized that the trade would help hockey penetrate the American market at its least logical orifice – Los Angeles, California, where ice is normally found only in strawberry daquiris. It's a little like trying to bring polo to Cleveland, and it proves beyond all doubt that realism is only a style, but no matter. Strachan didn't mention the daquiris, Cleveland, or alternate styles of writing, in case you were wondering.

On the same page, along with a profile of McNall, there was a wire service story quoting disgruntled former Oiler super-defenceman Paul Coffey as saying that, to Pocklington, Gretzky was just "a piece of meat" traded for hard cash. Coffey also pooh-poohed the theory that Janet Jones had anything to do with the trade. Former Oilers and Gretzky friends Dave Lumley and Ed Mio backed Coffey's opinion. Lumley reported that Pocklington, in order to cover his ass with the locals, had brow-beaten Gretzky into saying that he'd requested the trade.

A day or two later, Pocklington, in an effort to elude the growing heat in Edmonton for having traded God to the Global Village, put his foot firmly in the proverbial bucket. He explained to an Edmonton sportswriter that the Great One had been putting on an act at the press conference, and that if the truth were told, his former property has an ego the size of Manhattan and can hardly wait to get to the big city to exercise it.

If nothing else, Pocklington is a known expert on gigantic egos. So just for fun, or maybe because I can't resist a sitting duck, let's stop and take a little closer look at Peter Pocklington's ego and career.

Pocklington came to national prominence during the 1983 federal

Tory leadership race. He ran on an ultra-right-wing platform of unrestricted free enterprise, death to trade unions and anyone else without a job and a Mercedes-Benz, and reinstitution of the flat-earth cosmology. He's a former car salesman turned real estate speculator and hog butcher. He was dangerously close to the Fidelity Trust fiasco that stiffed the Canada Deposit Insurance Corporation for $200 million, and CDIC is still suing him for the return of funds that he removed from Fidelity before its collapse.

Currently Pocklington is chopping up 35,000 pigs a week in his Alberta Gainers operations. Gainers, incidentally, was the site of one of the most violent union-bashing episodes in recent Canadian labour history, an episode Pocklington came out of with $71.4 million in Alberta government modernization grants, loans and loan guarantees. He's been sued for $7 million by his private psychic, and was once held hostage by a gunman for eleven hours. Pocklington claims that he'd talked the gunman over to his free enterprise beliefs by the time the cops broke in and shot the culprit. A more probable scenario is that he talked the gunman into a coma, or suckerpunched him with a bribe and then ratted him out.

Even a Conservative Party camp follower can see from the above that Pocklington is a wonderful guy, and a leadership role model for when the sector of the population that believes Elvis is still alive and that Mulroney is a good prime minister runs out of Valium. Yet within days of the Gretzky trade, the citizens of Edmonton were burning Pocklington in effigy, planning boycotts of his various company's products, and Mayor Laurence Decore was organizing a plan to buy the Oilers from him. The Oiler players themselves were considering going on strike. Even the *Globe and Mail* was questioning Pocklington's abilities as a logician.

A few days after the trade and the revelations about Gretzky's alleged ego, *Globe* sports columnist Al Strachan wrote a piece that was somewhat critical of Pocklington, noting that "these allegations of Pocklington's are so far-fetched that one is almost forced to step back and wonder if it is fair to apply further criticism to a man who is so clearly out of touch with reality."

Unfortunately, Strachan himself didn't step back. The *Globe and Mail* editorial cops must have come in and beaten up on him at this point, because he concluded the column with his own stunning piece of illogic: "There is a temptation to try to defend Gretzky by carving up Pocklington, but Gretzky himself refuses to do that, so there's no reason for anyone else to do it." Strachan did not stop to note that our out-of-touch-with-reality Pocklington is $15 million richer, and has deprived Edmonton, Alberta, and all of Canada of an irreplaceable delight.

Neither, as far as I can see, has anyone else taken a further step back to look at what the Gretzky trade truly means. The Oiler players backed off on their threat, trade union reps cautioned against boycotting Pocklington's companies because it would hurt workers, and the public meeting organized to marshall support for purchasing the team fizzled.

So Wayne Gretzky goes off to Los Angeles, where he will do good works on behalf of the corporate fortunes of professional hockey. For himself, he'll no doubt make an extra couple of million annually from endorsements, of which Los Angeles is the acknowledged Mecca.

Meanwhile, the trade contains the following messages for Canadians, all of them part and parcel of a neoconservative litany that is the barely hidden subliminal message of the Free Trade Agreement:

1. Question: What runs the world?
   Answer: Money.
2. Question: Where's the money?
   Answer: New York and Los Angeles.
3. Question: Who controls the money?
   Answer: The corporate sector.
4. Question: What should we do about it?
   Answer: Roll over on our backs and let them hump us.

If you're trying to figure out what's going to happen to Canada when the Free Trade Agreement really gets into gear, the corporate sector of our national sport just gave us a perfect preview. No, I'm not being paranoid. And neither was MP Nelson Riis, when he got up in the House of Commons and said more or less the same thing. Peter Pocklington's trade of Wayne Gretzky to the Los Angeles Kings is a model of what's going to happen to all our irreplaceable assets under Free Trade. As Paul Coffey says, for free-trading folks like Peter Pocklington, we're nothing more than pieces of meat.

If I were Rick Salutin, I'd pack a suitcase. After he gets traded to *Saturday Night*, Conrad Black will probably ship him to the Los Angeles *Times* or to *T.V. Guide*. On the other hand, maybe we can get something for Robertson Davies. I hope it won't be Norman Mailer.

This Magazine

ORWELL OR
JAMES JOYCE

In the 20th century, futurology has become big business in ways that few people are aware of. Some of us will recall the silly Gyro Gearloose cities-of-the-future that used to appear on the back covers of comic books while we were growing up, and we might even notice that daytime radio, television and the tabloids are full of moronically optimistic pronouncements about oncoming products by professional technology-cheerleaders like Frank Ogden. While such pop futurology is pretty silly stuff, it shouldn't trick us into thinking that all futurology is inconsequential. Futurology has a side that is deadly serious, and it has gained an extraordinary degree of influence over our political and economic systems. Most of that influence, according to Max Dublin's brilliant analysis of this largely subliminal or covert industry, *FutureHype*, has been socially and culturally destructive. And it is an influence that is growing.

Max Dublin isn't this year's John Naisbitt, and *FutureHype* is not this year's version of *Megatrends*. In fact, the book is a much-needed antidote to the recent deluge of futurology tomes that instruct us on everything from how to cash in on economic chaos to how to induce moral and intellectual comas in the face of nuclear insanity. Dublin, with Joyce Nelson, is among the few serious cybernetic thinkers to emerge in Canada since Marshall McLuhan.

Unlike the often flighty McLuhan, Dublin sets out to detect the lineaments of the present crisis, not to unfold the grand scheme of the future. His research is remarkably untrammelled (and untrampled) by sacred cattle – a rare delight in itself – and the range of his knowledge is wide and heterodox. Yet the erudition is unobtrusive, as befits a man who looks to George Orwell rather than James Joyce (who was McLuhan's master) for his intellectual method.

FutureHype begins by outlining the pathological side of futurology by examining its psychological and ideological bases, both in the West and in the Soviet bloc. In tracing it back to a common root in Hegel's impulse to eliminate contingency, Dublin is no kinder to Marxism's strain of futurology than to our own. From there, he looks at the effects of futurological thinking in its three most influential spheres of activity: education, health and military planning. In the rather frightening section on military planning, he demonstrates with startling clarity that madness and logic are not enemies but twins. As a bonus, his arguments charbroil futurologists like Henry Kissinger and Herman Kahn without mercy, although he doesn't, unfortunately, reveal which of these latter-day Gearlooses was the model for Doctor Strangelove. The analyses of educational and health futurology are no less penetrating but they are slightly less frightening.

Here's the basic argument of *FutureHype*, with apologies to the author for attempting to summarize an enormously rich and complex text in so short a space: At the core of all futurology, Dublin argues, is first and foremost a logic, and an essentially brainless proclivity toward worshipping the exclusionary powers that logical fulfilment offers. What we are trading, in our enthusiasm for futurology, is our capacity to integrate contingencies and to make the humane contextualizations on which civilized behaviour has always depended.

"Prophecy today," Dublin writes, "can be regarded as being no more than an attempt by self-appointed experts to rationalize the future, along with everything else under the sun. Rationalization today has become little more than an attempt to order and control just about everything by pressing it into the mold of formal logic, and into the paltry calculus of formal means geared toward the achievement of what usually turn out to be extremely narrow ends. In the process of trying to fit everything into this mold, we are constantly deluding ourselves about what can and cannot be done."

Most of the predictions that have dominated social, economic and military planning over the last four decades have been binary extrapolations of what is already visibly happening. Nearly always the predictions have been simple extrapolations of short-term trends, and sometimes they have been logarithmic extrapolations. They're also a dangerously aggressive and inhumane kind of stupidity, and their power tends to engender the same in us. They encourage us to live in an artifically narrow future, moving us from the complexities of the present to exploit short-term opportunities that have a demonstrated tendency to blow up in our collective and individual faces when tomorrow actually arrives. Dublin concludes that "The attack on human freedom by modern prophecy is perhaps the most disturbing aspect of futurology. Squeezed between the 'terror of history' and the 'tyranny of prophecy', people today . . . find they have little room to manoeuvre. No wonder our prophets appeal, as Orwell observed, to our fear and our craving for power: these are precisely the drives that dominate those who feel trapped."

Dublin is himself a prophet, but he is anything but a futurologist. In the Old Testament, prophets were usually slightly crazed and cranky outsiders who excoriated the tribe for their sinfulness and lack of foresight, and made dire predictions about what would happen if they didn't clean up their act. Among them, the prophet Jeremiah was the crankiest, but he was also perhaps the best informed. He was fond of sitting atop the hills overlooking the encampment, a vantage point that allowed him to see the idiotic behaviour of his compatriots, and, off in the distance, the smoke and dust of the oncoming barbarians.

That pretty much describes Dublin's positioning. Yet *FutureHype* is considerably more than a jeremiad. For all his brilliance and insight into a dangerous situation, Dublin exercises a profound sense of humour, and at key points in his arguments he has the good instinct to expose what is ridiculous with wit and laughter, albeit without letting anyone or anything off his hook. The result is a highly readable book that is of great penetration and urgency.

As a former urban planner, I'd recommend this book as compulsory reading for anyone involved in the profession, either as a student or functionary. I suspect *FutureHype*'s pertinence to other professions, given the general crisis of method our society is mired in, is equally crucial. For the general reader, at whom the book is accurately and accessibly aimed, there is a wealth of insights about our society no one else has gotten quite as clearly.

New Directions / Books in Canada

NOT FORGETTING CAMBODIA

In June 1978, at an isolated agricultural commune in Battambang province in Northwestern Cambodia, a man was forced to watch his pregnant wife die in his arms. The man was a medical doctor, but if this had been known to commune authorities it would have meant torture and death for him, his wife, and every other member of his family. He did not, therefore, perform the simple medical manoeuvre that would have saved her life. The man's name was Haing Ngor.

Most people know Haing Ngor as the Oscar-winning actor in 1985's *The Killing Fields*. He played the role of Dith Pran, the Cambodian assistant *New York Times* journalist Sidney Schanberg abandoned when the victorious Khmer Rouge entered Phnom Penh in 1975. Dith survived several years as a Khmer Rouge war slave before escaping to Thailand.

The Killing Fields was a excellent film, and Haing reenacted the experiences of Dith Pran with a kind of authenticity and intensity that made me wonder what his own story was. Now, with American journalist Roger Warner, he has written an autobiography. It is called *Haing Ngor: A Cambodian Odyssey*, and in many ways, it is an even more remarkable story than Dith Pran's.

When the Khmer Rouge entered Phnom Penh in April 1975, Haing was a Phnom Penh gynecologist of mixed Khmer and Chinese descent. Unlike Dith Pran, and like the majority of the Cambodian middle class, until the Khmer Rouge arrived he had been doing his best to ignore the war going on around him. He was both protected and blinded by his private ambitions and privileges, and he had no more than an inkling of what was to come.

To come was a nightmare that lasted almost four years for Haing, and is still going on for the majority of Cambodians. The Khmer Rouge used Cambodia's several million-strong urban and refugee population as the labour component for one of the most crazed social and economic experiments this century has seen. What they invented was a new strain of genocide, in which anyone who was not indige- nously "Khmer" – a term applied very capriciously by the Khmer Rouge leadership – was sentenced to death. That meant, in practice, that the entire urban population – "new people" in the Khmer Rouge argot – was forced into the countryside to produce rice, and to work on vast and generally ill-conceived irrigation and land-reclamation projects – and to die. There they faced two fundamental choices: slow death by overwork, malnutrition or disease, or a swifter death by execution at the hands of their Khmer Rouge masters. That may sound like an exaggeration, but Pol Pot, the Khmer Rouge leader, is said to have remarked that Cambodia needed just one million people to renew the ancient Khmer empire. When he said it, there were nearly seven million Cambodians under his control.

Those with a stomach strong enough to check this out should have a look at *Pol Pot Plans the Future: Confidential Leadership Docu- ments from Democratic Kampuchea, 1976-1977*, translated and edited by David P. Chandler, Ben Kiernan, and Chanthou Boua.

We should all know who Pol Pot was and what he had in mind, because he is still with us. The most recent reports I've heard have him living comfortably in a military hideaway near Trat, Thailand, planning the reconquest of Cambodia. Despite reports to the contrary, he remains the undisputed leader of the Communist Party of Kampuchea. He is the braintrust of Angka, the xenophobic party clique that was responsible for the genocidal massacres of 1975-79. He is no doubt thinking still of how to defeat the "deeply hidden and unnoticed" forces that he believes undermined his regime.

Who are these "forces" he's so paranoid about? Pretty much the same ones he attempted to exterminate while Angka was carrying out its 44-month bloodbath: Cambodians of Vietnamese, Cham, Chinese, or Montagnard descent, party officials close enough to the Vietnamese border to have been accused of being tainted by that moderating proximity, anyone who had ever lived in an urban area, those who were educated, who could read or write, or had Western technical training (however slight), and finally, the one or two people in the country who might actually have been working for the CIA or the KGB. To Pol Pot, all of the above were agents of "foreign powers" that might have sullied the purity of his Khmer Rouge utopia.

Along with Ieng Sary, Khieu Samphan, and a small coterie of similarly paranoid and xenophobic Maoists, Pol Pot planned and carried out a program of political and cultural mayhem that completed the destruction of Cambodia begun with the illegal 1970 invasion by American troops and the illegal three-year carpet bombing of the Cambodian countryside that saw more tons of explosives dropped on this small agrarian nation than the Allied Forces dropped on Nazi Germany during World War II.

Unfortunately for the Cambodian people, the Khmer Rouge programs, which were aimed primarily at their urban population, fall outside the United Nations' *Realpolitik* definitions of genocide. The UN definitions confine the acceptable definition of genocide to sociological parameters based on the race and religion of the victims and ignores the issue of the political intent of the perpetrators. The definition is unfortunate for a variety of fairly obvious reasons. It

was created to protect Stalinist Russia from being accused of genocide over its actions in the Ukraine and for the purges of the late
1930s, but the inadequate parameters of those definitional articles
have since kept the Khmer Rouge and a number of other regimes
from facing censure within the UN and elsewhere, and have made
millions of innocent people – not just in Cambodia – expendable
pawns of Cold War geopolitics.

In Cambodia, the result is that the Khmer Rouge still sit in the UN
General Assembly as the legitimate political representatives of Cambodia, and are accorded military or diplomatic support by the majority of Western governments, including our own. It also helps to perpetuate the immoral geopolitical myopia that has those same governments insisting on Khmer Rouge participation in any political
restructuring of the country. As a matter of record, External Affairs
Minister Joe Clark repeatedly suggested just that as part of Canada's
general boot-licking compliance with American foreign policy.

No competent analyst of Cambodia has gone along with such proposals, and few are likely to in the future. They know what will happen if the Khmer Rouge remain an internationally legitimate – and
armed – political force within the country. Now, the United States,
presumably bowing to public opinion in the face of successfully
renewed Khmer Rouge aggression, seems prepared to withdraw its
support and offer tentative support for the Vietnamese-backed government. It is a step in the right direction, but not yet a decisive one.
Since 1975 the United States has treated anyone (and any government) connected with Vietnam as if they were not members of the
human species. With its renewed status as a superpower, the U.S. is
likely to have a hard time giving up its grudge against the only nation
that has ever defeated it on the battlefield.

Students and functionaries of global *Realpolitik* will know all
about the egotism of U.S. foreign policy, but they might understand
the situation better – and the reason for the intractable opposition
elsewhere to the Khmer Rouge – if they were to read Boua, Chandler
and Kiernan's judicious compilation of Khmer Rouge organizational

documents and plans. The authors have let Pol Pot and his associates reveal the degree to which genocidal lunacy can be rationalized and organized, and they show, with the inclusion of the translation of one of the many torture-induced confessions written by the Khmer Rouge's political victims, the psychotic savagery to which the regime resorted.

By the time the Vietnamese invaded the country in early 1979, the Khmer Rouge had exterminated between a million and two million people, most of them "new people" like Haing Ngor and his family. In an utterly different way than the translated Khmer Rouge documents, Haing Ngor's recounting of the destruction of Cambodia has the unmistakable ring of authenticity. He suffered irrationally brutal treatment, losing his wife, parents, and most of the rest of his family – 33 of 42. As a medical doctor, he was automatically under a death sentence, and had to hide his identity. Still, he was tortured three times for various minor ideological errors. He eluded execution through a combination of strength of character and sheer chance. Few who ran afoul of the Khmer Rouge survived a single encounter.

Not surprisingly, what emerges from his book is a portrait of an extremely strong and intelligent man who survived because of a complex mix of cunning, will, and Buddhist quietism. Equally important, Haing provides us with a unique portrait of Cambodian society before, during, and after the Khmer Rouge had done their worst. Despite his obvious rage and sorrow, he is able to assign the blame for what happened in Cambodia with startling judiciousness. He damns the Americans for the CIA overthrow of the neutralist Sihanouk government in 1970, and for the irreparable damage to the country's economic and social fabric caused by the 1969 invasion and subsequent bombing. Nor is he any easier on the Vietnamese, who invaded the country and suppressed the Khmer Rouge, and then imposed an only slightly more palatable, if considerably less violent, brand of authoritarian control over a nation that has never asked to be controlled by anybody.

Haing's primary subject matter, however, is the Khmer Rouge

years, and his recounting of his experiences under their control occupies the bulk of the book. He does not, as might be expected, simply blame it on communism. Instead, he cites a combination of factors – the longstanding hostility between Cambodia's urban and rural populations, the dislocation of war, geopolitical idiocy, the xenophobic Maoism of the Khmer Rouge's ruling group, and the uniquely Khmer concept of *kum* that creates a society obsessed with saving face and obtaining revenge.

Although he did not know who Pol Pot was during the time he was under Khmer Rouge control, Haing Ngor provides a brief chapter about him that is probably the most concise summary of the psychotic nature of the man and his regime yet recorded.

Given the recent Vietnamese withdrawal from Cambodia, and given the complexity of the ongoing national reconciliation process – itself as much the result of the indifference and venality of the international community as the result of the intransigence of the Cambodian factions – both these books are important and timely.

Cambodia seems on the verge of becoming Southeast Asia's Lebanon. Its dimensions and violence, however, will make Lebanon seem like an afternoon picnic. If the killing of innocent Cambodians continues, unneccessary ignorance – ours and that of our political leaders – will once again be a powerful contributor. In the welter of current events it is all too easy to forget Cambodia. But the torture of this once-peaceful nation has now entered its third decade, and shows no reliable signs of ending. More than Lebanon or Latin America, Cambodia is a painful illustration of how crazy the world has gotten, both in the astonishing brutalities it has suffered and in the maniacal geopolitical agendas that continue to compete for control within Cambodia's borders and within the human heart.

Toronto Star / Canadian Forum

NOAM CHOMSKY AND THE 'ACTUAL RECORD'

There is something about Noam Chomsky that has bothered me for a long time, but which I haven't quite had the occasion or the courage to pin down. You see, I don't trust him.

That's heresy, I know. A blue ribbon panel at the CBC selected him to present the 1988 Massey Lectures, and every right-minded person from the political centre and left in North America believes his pronouncements are gospel truth. So what possible uneasiness could I legitimately have?

Well, let's begin by enumerating Noam Chomsky's strengths. He is brilliant and articulate, both as a linguistic theorist and as the most strident and persistent critic of American foreign policy over the last two decades. He's a fellow of the American Academy of Arts and Sciences, and a member of the National Academy of Science and of the Arts and Sciences. He's currently an Institute Professor at MIT where he teaches linguistics and philosophy – their house communist, sort of. In short, Noam Chomsky is everything this side of Santa

Claus. He has had every privilege and honour the United States offers to intellectuals conferred upon him. Indeed, it is a privilege to be able to read his books and to listen to him on the radio.

Have another look, this time at his intellectual method. His judgments, even in his early writings on linguistic deep structures, have carried an extremist's air of utter certainty, as if their sheer brilliance and horsepower had swept away all other possibilities prior to articulation. They, and Chomsky, are singularly unhumble and untentative. Don't argue with me, his demeanor implies, I've got everything covered and I'm right.

Whenever I read Chomsky, I get the impression that I'm in the presence of a man and a mind that has never known a moment of confusion or been caught in a contradiction. His discourse is always sleek and effortless and perfect, an elemental rebuke to all other views of his chosen subject matter and to all other methods of securing it, a slap in the face to ambiguity, circumspection and the bumbling doggedness with which most people – including myself – pursue the truth. When Noam Chomsky awakens in the morning, he knows exactly where in the universe he is, and what he's going to do in – and to – the world. He knows exactly where American foreign policy is at, and how it is different from that of Russia or China or North Vietnam or the Republic of Chad. I suspect that he knows exactly where his leotards are, and whether he's going to put on green or black or red ones. His way of doing things implies, even though we know better, that he doesn't have to put them on one leg at a time.

Other powerful minds in our century haven't had that kind of certitude. There is nothing in Chomsky of, say, Samuel Beckett, who had to make a conscious, laboured decision about whether to even get out of bed in the morning. There is nothing in Chomsky of Albert Camus' moral agony, no choice to be made between competing elements of existence for a stake in the truth, no creeping doubt lurking in the black and white of print nor any invasive darkness in the grey morning air over a beloved city. In Chomsky's prose there is nothing of, say, John Berger's excruciatingly laboured struggles to claim the texture of human intellection from its – and his – inarticulate natural state. Chomsky's universe is morally unclouded and unerringly logical. His judgments about friend and foe alike are direct and unbending. Get out of this man's way because he's right and you're wrong – unless you already agree with him.

Nothing I've said so far is a denial of the general brilliance or even the accuracy of Chomsky's analytical powers, or of the well-researched and penetrating truths of his many pronouncements concerning the evil of American imperialism. Many have been inspired insights, and as far as I know, they've only carried him into one major error. That error, however, was a serious one. Chomsky supported the Khmer Rouge government of Cambodia for some time after nearly everyone else in the world (including everyone in the political left except the Maoists) recognized that the Khmer Rouge were a brutal Stalinist lunacy that not only lost control of their murderous impulses on a mass scale, but never had a coherent method in the first place.

As an analyst of Cambodia I was deeply angered by Chomsky's support, and I followed his cavilling retraction from his original supportive position very carefully. He withdrew in the manner of a military force withdrawing reluctantly from a physical territory – strategically and without any substantive admission of error or show of vulnerability or remorse. His fall-back position was revealing and perhaps typical. The Khmer Rouge psychosis of 1975-79, in his revised opinion, was purely the product of the brutal U.S. bombing of Cambodia that ended in 1973. At no point did he attempt to account for the excesses of the regime on its own terms, even though the evidence makes it clear that what took place was as much a product of the Leninist model of political organization and authority as a psychotic overreaction to U.S. actions. The unconscionable and brutal U.S. bombing may have created the Khmer Rouge field cadres, but the paranoiac (and Western-trained Maoist) vanguard clustered around Pol Pot told them what to do, and how.

●

All this is a preface for why I come to a book like Chomsky's *The Culture of Terrorism* somewhat warily, unwilling to bend to the logical sleekness and partiality that are the author's trade marks. I know that I'll agree with most of what he says, but I'm determined not to let his brilliance convince me to enter into an emotional collusion with an exclusionary vision of the world. And before I go further, let me reiterate that in this volume as elsewhere, Noam Chomsky is a brilliant analyst, and is generally accurate in his research and in his judgments. *The Culture of Terrorism* is a penetrating analysis of American foreign policy and practice in Central America and it should be read. But the issue I'm pursuing is about what his overbearing rhetoric and his demonology excludes and/or adds.

The first thing I discover is that this book is not quite about what the title suggests it will be. I always thought terrorism was an extrapartisan phenomena forged in the revolutionary crucible of the Soviet Union early in this century, and fine-tuned by Nazi Germany. It bifurcated further in the atmosphere of the Cold War, and reached its present character in the covert social and economic impoverishment that has taken place in the Third World just as much of it was gaining apparent political independence. In *The Culture of Terrorism* Chomsky is talking solely about the state terrorism inherent in U.S. foreign policy, focusing chiefly on recent U.S. attempts to destabilize Nicaragua. It is an interesting subject matter, and a major explication of an important strain of terrorism. But it is *not* the paradigm of all terrorism, and the book's title is therefore misleading.

I read Chomsky's preface to the book, as I have taught myself to, not only as a statement of his intentions but also as an exercise in rhetorical management. Chomsky, like any other logician, is a master of shaping the context of his discourse by setting the terms in rhetorical concrete. The preface and introduction to *The Culture of Terrorism* are masterpieces of rhetorical and logical distortion.

Let's take the first paragraph of the first essay and examine it sentence by sentence. Here's the first: "The scandals that erupted in the Fall of 1986 and the reaction to them cast a revealing light on the political system and the intellectual culture that interprets and sustains it." The "scandals" refer to the Irangate revelations in which Oliver North and friends were found to be selling arms to Iran and diverting the money to the Nicaraguan Contras – with or without the conscious knowledge of President Reagan (whose presidency rendered the concept of full executive consciousness meaningless anyway). My personal view is that the Irangate events were criminal acts rather than scandals, ones that throughout were more prone to slither than erupt. Likewise, I'm unconvinced that there was any kind of coherent media and judicial reaction to them, other than the kind reptiles have to threatening movement, and that they revealed very little about American political life except that we are a long way beyond Watergate, and that the slimeballs learned from it.

Despite the loaded nouns and the fudging adjectives, that sentence has nothing on the succeeding one: "As we shall see in detail below, these events demonstrated that the United States remains dedicated to the rule of force, that political elites agree and indeed insist that it must remain so, and that, furthermore, the commitment to violence and lawlessness frames their self-image as well, barely concealed beneath deceptive rhetoric." This is an interesting sentence. It begins with a "don't argue with me because I'm going to bury you with facts" admonition, and then commences to paint the entire governmental structure of the United States as a series of interconnected mafias self-consciously dedicating themselves to mayhem and crime. I'm no fan of the United States – particularly not its foreign policy and military preoccupations – but this does seems excessive. If I agree to the verity of Chomsky's description of the U.S., I've committed myself to a Standard Total View (STV) of the U.S. as a demonic purveyor of more or less total evil. There are some rainy days when I might be tempted to believe this, but Chomsky has hung a curious rider to it I can't abide – that the Americans know they're evil, and that they cultivate it behind a rhetorical screen.

At this point, Chomsky's third sentence clamps itself around my brain like a steel strap: "These conclusions can readily be drawn from the actual record, if we face it honestly and without illusion." Now,

Chomsky and I are of course in favour of facing things honestly and without illusion, and so are you, right? That being the case, we should by now be gathered atop his rhetorical wave, ready to crash down among the heathen dishonesties and creepoids and make our conclusions drawn from the "actual record".

I'm going to stop here, without finishing my analysis of the paragraph, and do a *mea culpa*. This is pretty bitchy stuff I'm doing, and it isn't at all fair. I'd be the first to admit that it is impossible to write anything without a divisible rhetoric. But page after page of Chomsky's books are crudded with the sort of bullying, single-minded rhetorical persuasion I excerpted. In isolation from the factual materials he offers up in bulk, he's as much a fucked-up fundamentalist and moral bully as are Herbert W. Armstrong's ghost writers.

So there are two things about Chomsky I don't like, really. First, I don't like being manipulated or pushed around. Whether it is the McDonald's Corporation or Noam Chomsky turning my head makes no difference, except that it is even less pleasant to be manipulated by your allies than by your enemies. Most of us, by now, are aware of the motives of the McDonald's Corporation. They want us to head down to the Golden Arches for a McBLT and they'd like us to order the large fries while we're there, because that's the item that they make the greatest profit from. But what about Chomsky? Doesn't he trust us to figure things out on the basis of the analytical figures and facts he presents? Apparently not. If he did, I don't think he'd demand that we submit to what he's called the "actual record".

The idea of an "actual record" is one that the history of the 20th century, with its myriad erasures and revisions of fact and truth should have taught anyone with more than about 35 cards in their deck to view with skepticism. There is, quite simply, no such thing as the "actual record", just as there is no such thing as a simple fact. This is a century of lies, tricks, misinformation and cartoons, and anyone who tries to convince us to participate in something called the "actual record", even if he's acting in what he believes is our best interest, isn't to be accorded our complete trust.

That's a very hard thing to believe about Chomsky, because of his sincerity and because he is so thorough. Perhaps that thoroughness is part of the problem. In *The Culture of Terrorism* and elsewhere, he conducts a closed discourse, and the rhetorical net he slings across each and every page is nearly seamless. It is so nearly seamless that it is hard to see that Chomsky is almost Oedipally focused on an exclusive strain of malfeasance in the world – that of U.S. foreign policy. What we're being asked to accept as the "actual record" is not that at all, but a record that is defined, at least in part, by Chomsky's neurosis about the United States government.

I don't like the fundamentalism implicit in that single focus. It misses too many things, such as the malfeasance of Russian, Chinese and, in the case of *The Culture of Terrorism*, Sandinista foreign policy. More important finally, it also ignores the factors of stupidity and incompetence, which, as far as I can see, are a more consistent and evident strain in American foreign policy than the organized conspiracy of evil maniacs Chomsky believes is running the show.

I may be blinding myself with my dislike of fundamentalist thinking here, of course. But my reason for disliking fundamentalists (wherever I find them) is a sound one. Fundamentalists always believe in the absolute intelligence of evil, and in the equally absolute vulnerability of good – except, of course, their own.

I'd argue that life works the other way round. Evil is stupid and incompetent, and good is by nature intelligent and sanguine – and generous. The vulnerability of good derives from its inherently curious and unparanoiac nature. Curiosity rarely lends itself to a single focus because it is interested in everything, and its lack of paranoia makes it hesitant to align itself with partisan viewpoints, even if they are contiguous, for defensive or power-gathering purposes. This is a roundabout way of saying I may just be irritable at having truth force-fed to me the way Chomsky does it – that it makes me distrustful. And you'll notice that I'm not trying to ram this down your throat as if it were the sole truth about Chomsky, which is a courtesy you'll never get from him while he's in the full ecstasy of an investigative track.

I do agree with him that the American economic and foreign policy

apparatuses probably are the chief threat to continued human survival on this planet – which is a highfalutin' way of saying that I
agree with his belief that we're the baddest bad guys in this world.
But I don't think it is because America is inherently evil, just that it
wields the most power and devours the greatest part of the planet's
diminishing resources to feed its gluttonous appetites. To present the
various American political apparatuses as a coherent and self-consciously evil monolith is a gross exaggeration of reality and a breakdown of intellectual method. However bad the U.S. has become, it
still ain't Nazi Germany, and it isn't Stalinist Russia. If it was, Noam
Chomsky would have been silenced a long time ago. Come to think
of it, if Chomsky were a Nicaraguan, the Sandinistas probably would
have tried to stuff a gag in his mouth by now.

Look. Humane reality is more than merely a logical net in which
ideas and people are to be entrapped. If it sometimes appears to be, it
is because the observer hasn't examined the fabric fully. The truth of
any given situation or subject matter is a seamy network of ideas and
events that intelligent people can (and must) pick apart so that the
poisonous spiders of logic fall from their perches and so that the
goodies – the glory of complex ideas and things – come tumbling
out. Partisan coherence and logical enclosure are the building materials of the spiders, not tools of humane analysis.

I'm not asking Chomsky to shut up. I just want him to clean up his
act a little, admit that there are some questions he doesn't have the
answers to, and to respect the intelligence of his readers more.
Maybe he should take a two-week vacation with someone like P.J.
O'Rourke, who has recently given us some extraordinarily clear
glimpses of the geopolitical net by refusing to do anything else but
pick at those bulging seams I spoke of. He could show Noam Chomsky a few things about what an "actual record" looks like, and how it
operates. Meanwhile, do read *The Culture of Terrorism*. But read it
very, very carefully.

Books in Canada

A LARGE AND
IMPORTANT LIFE

Harvest House, a small and not very together Canadian press, recently published a modest-looking little book titled *Life Begins at 65: The Not Entirely Candid Autobiography of a Drifter*, by Hans Blumenfeld. It is not what it appears to be, this book. It has very little to do with old age, and it does not have an obscure or inconsequential reminiscence anywhere in it. It is one of those rare books that manages to be edifying and entertaining at the same time, mainly because Hans Blumenfeld is among the twenty or thirty most interesting men to have lived in Canada in this century.

I met Blumenfeld just once, during the mid-1970s in Vancouver. He'd been brought to Vancouver by then-Regional Planning Director Harry Lash to add his wisdom to Lash's $5-million metropolitan plan for Greater Vancouver. My recollection of him is of a small, abrasively confident man with a heavy German accent who argued with everything and everyone. Unfortunately I recall only the effortless way he raised the hackles of the planners he was there to advise.

What he was telling them went right over my head. As one of a group of wild-eyed radicals Lash hired from a variety of academic backgrounds to find out what kind of city the public wanted, I was very much on the periphery of the planning department and of the discussions with Blumenfeld. Lash had hired me because I understood and wrote English quite well, and he therefore astutely encouraged me to remain untainted by the obtuse jargon urban planners talked in.

At the time, I sensed that I was missing something profound, but it wasn't until I read Blumenfeld's autobiography that I began to seriously regret my inattention. I had been in the company of a truly remarkable and wise man.

The least informative thing about either the autobiography or the life of this extraordinary world citizen is the title that was chosen for his book. It is probably the only thing in the book Blumenfeld didn't author. Publication was partially funded by a grant from the Canadian Institute of Planners, and consequently the volume is framed as if it was of interest only to urban planners. As is usually the case when urban planners make decisions about what the public can understand or ought to know about, the editors were wrong. The book – and Blumenfeld's life – are of much wider interest than they have recognized.

Certainly, his long career (he died recently in his mid-90s) didn't begin at 65. It only marks the age at which he arrived in Canada to work with Murray V. Jones in Metro Toronto's infant planning department. Note that I used the term *work with*. Blumenfeld didn't work *under* anybody or anything in his entire life. He worked with an astonishing range of this century's most talented urban designers, architects and planners, and in a wide variety of locations and political circumstances, including seven years spent in the Soviet Union during the 1930s.

What Blumenfeld worked *for* is still more interesting, both for its content and for the consistency with which he pursued it. He believed that it is possible to create human settlements that are humane, efficient and based on social cooperation. Unfortunately for all of us, too many of today's intellectually and morally bankrupt planners just wave away such goals as utopian, content merely to engage their training and skills as a reactionary form of internal diplomacy.

Yet one would be hard-pressed to argue that Blumenfeld's career was that of an impractical dreamer. He was a life-long socialist and a technical pragmatist, and he argues throughout, and particularly in his insightful summing up chapter, that any competent urban planner must embrace those values together if humane and just cities have any hope of being achieved. And along the way, he supplies ample illustration as to why this is so, particularly in the chapters on Weimar Germany and the Soviet Union, which are the most tragically resolved experiments in human civil design ever attempted. Weimar resulted in Nazi Germany, and we are now seeing the full and detailed results of the disastrous Soviet experiment for the first time.

The book is a record of both his political and professional activities – between which he recognizes no difference. The caveat lodged in the subtitle – that the book is not entirely candid – is therefore accurate enough. Not much is revealed about his personal life beyond a few cryptic notes on his sexual relationships and one hilarious anecdote about a short and ill-fated fling as a patient of psychoanalyst Alfred Adler, the spiritual grandfather of Scientology, EST and a lot of other bogus self-help therapies. I'm sure that the details of his private life would be almost as interesting as his professional life, but Blumenfeld has more important fish to fry, and the recipes he reveals are far more profound than the gossipy business of who did what, to whom, and why.

Some of the things he has to tell us about planning and about our cities are distinctly unfashionable now that we are drowning both our urban ecosystems and our political economy in entrepreneurial drool. Personally I was disturbed by his enthusiasm for the Soviet Union, particularly his non-explanation of the Ukraine famine, which he witnessed at first hand in 1932 without benefit of the historical record to tell him that an administratively generated famine was taking place. But elsewhere in the volume, he is always challenging and in most instances, startlingly articulate.

A drifter, however, he was not. In the deepest sense, Hans Blumenfeld was a world citizen, one who managed to be at home – alert to local conditions and of use – wherever he lived. He knew where he'd been, and he had some very firm ideas about where we're going that are worth listening to today, now that he's gone. If this man was drifting, god help the rest of his profession.

Books in Canada

AN UNOFFICIAL DESIGN HISTORY OF EXPO 86

or, How Disney Redesigned Greater Vancouver

Nobody really knows exactly where and when the idea of Expo 86 was born, or from whose mind it was, er, hatched. Probably some mid-level bureaucrat at a privatization pep rally was demonstrating to a senior official how neoconservatively he or she could think, and a low-level chain reaction set in, sort of like a bacterial infection creating a plague of boils. If just one sensible person had said go soak your head, the public debt in B.C. would be a billion dollars lighter, and Expo 86 would not have happened.

The rationale for holding an exposition in British Columbia, and the theme that was chosen for it, are murkier still. Of course, strange things often happen in Western Canada when the spiral to riches is interrupted. In the 1930s, for instance, it bred Social Credit. Megalomaniacal public projects aren't exactly unheard of in B.C., either. Social Credit first got itself elected in 1952 on the coat-tails of a Swedish proposal to build a 500-mile monorail that was somehow supposed to open up the vast resources of the northern interior. The old-line parties were too sensible to fall for such obvious malarkey, but Social Credit and B.C.'s lunatic fringe (which is almost as extensive as the natural resources) bought into it without a second thought. Since then, successive Socred regimes have specialized in wild development schemes, laissez-faire treatment of the corporate resource extraction giants, and red scares. They have also inflicted one megaproject after another on the B.C. environment. The decision to go ahead with an urban megaproject like Expo 86, not surprisingly, was made in the aftermath of the worst economic downturn since the 1930s, and it too promised a monorail — even if this one was only 500 yards long.

Maybe it was the thought of finally getting their monorail that did it, but from the first moment, Expo seemed to warm the hearts of the Socreds. The somewhat spotted history of expositions indicates a logical, if untapped, affinity with the things Social Credit has always cherished. Both Social Credit and expositions have been, from their beginnings, vast conceptual gee-whiz gadgets.

The first expositions, before the turn of the century, were spectacular statements of optimism about the powers of civilization and technology. When the First World War demonstrated that civilized men could build deep trenches and then use technology to kill millions of combatants in them, there was a lull in the festivities. The 1939 Fair in New York City tried to revive the old spirit, but as we now know, the real spirit of the times was about to crawl out of the trenches and invade Poland.

The expository elan didn't really surface again until 1954, when it celebrated the rebirth of Europe at Brussels. The post-war expositions that followed were different for a while, too. The technocrats were still there to push product and productivity, but the enthusiasms were more circumspect about technology, and there was more emphasis on the ability of (or was it merely the need for) humane governments to enhance the quality of life and to keep us talking and dancing so that we didn't blow ourselves up with nuclear weapons. Whatever the motives, this phase reached its pinnacle in 1967 in Montreal, where the theme was Guys and Their World.

By the early 1980s, however, the Cold War was at its peak, privatization was on the upsurge, governments were trying to make themselves invisible, and the expositions were back to razzle-dazzle technology and how to get a better fuck for the buck. Expo 86 was designated as a class II (or theme) exposition, and the theme chosen was transportation and communications – how fast we can go, and how slick and shiny guys can make their rockets. What relevance this theme has to British Columbia, which has a small and mordant ship-building industry and hasn't built a vehicle with wheels on it since chuckwagons became obsolete, evidently slipped by the conceptual planners. The obvious alternate theme, given B.C.'s abundance and variety of natural resources, was to expostulate on how diligently we are clearcutting our forests and fouling our waters. The decision to concentrate on a locally irrelevant theme was no doubt influenced by how abysmally we have handled the things that are relevant to us.

What made B.C.'s Social Credit government agree to fund an exposition in downtown Vancouver is considerably clearer. They saw it as a means of securing a powerful megaproject presence within Vancouver's core. Since the early 1970s, Vancouver city governments had been moving slowly and steadily to the left, and were taking political positions that were increasingly in fundamental opposition to the Socred megaproject mentality. The Socreds therefore purchased a large block of land on the north shore of False Creek from Marathon Realty (then Canadian Pacific's development arm), and formed two crown corporations: B.C. Place Corporation to assemble land for the exposition, and the Expo 86 Corporation to build and run the exposition. Both were secretly aimed at screwing up Vancouver and its leftist administrations.

The Expo board of directors – headed by multi-millionaire entrepreneur and born-again Christian Jim Pattison – went out and hired a local architect, Bruno Freschi, as its chief architect. He was given whatever minimal conceptual parameters the management team had in their possession, no real budget limitations, and some slightly more concrete physical parameters to work with. "Design!" he was told.

For about a year, Freschi and the group of designers he hired to help him did just that. But Freschi's designs, when they came in, were somewhat fantastical for the sober-minded Expo board. More damaging, they were outrageously expensive, even for a megaproject. Freschi was rapped on the knuckles and pushed to the design sidelines, although he remained, officially, the chief architect of Expo 86 through to the end. His substantive contribution to the site is the Expo Centre (now Science World, and not always affectionately known as the Golfball), a fake geodesic dome covered by flashing lights that sits at the east end of the site. Even that building is greatly reduced from its original conception.

Freschi also laid out the rough conceptual blueprint for the Expo site. After he was kneecapped, four basic groups accounted for the design of the fair. These groups are quite distinct in character, mandate and ambition.

1. **The contract architects:** This group consisted of the twenty-five or thirty architectural firms that designed most of the individual buildings on the fair site. The majority of those firms were local, although more than a few of them brought in exposition-experienced help for specific tasks. The architects were assigned portions of the site on an ad hoc basis, thus bypassing the more conventional "design panel" selection of proposals one might have expected. As a result, they accounted for the most interesting buildings of the fair. Sounds great, until we recall that there *weren't* any interesting buildings.

2. **The Expo design teams:** There were a number of these. They were constantly being blown apart and then reconstituted, and there were lots of summary executions along the way. After Freschi was removed, a second wave of designers and architects, headed by Richard Blagborne, tried to find an interface between Freschi's grand ambitions and the limitations laid down by increasingly powerful budget-management teams. In that stifling environment, they carried out the bulk of the site design.

A startling amount of this work was carried out in-house by young and generally poorly paid graduate architects who were hired for short periods, drained of their creative energies, and then fired. Some big-name architects were brought in, the most prominent of which was New Yorker James Wines, who was hired to produce Highway 86, the monochromatic set-piece of the Expo site.

Finally, after Blagborne was carried off in one of the Expo board's administrative massacres, another wave of designers, headed by creative director Ron Woodall and Vancouver architect John Perkins, did the site embellishment that ultimately was the sole element in the entire fair design that made any attempt to integrate the different components.

Blagborne, Woodall and particularly Perkins did some brilliant and courageous work in an increasingly hostile conceptual and budgetary environment. They also provided about the only explanations of the design process that have emerged. As a class II exposition, they explained, Expo was not primarily an architectural exposition. On other occasions, they argued somewhat cryptically that Expo was a post-architectural exposition, a designation that may yet turn out to be prophetic in ways they didn't dream of, given the CAD-based technologies that are dissolving the barrier between the Magic Kingdom and commercial architecture by eradicating creativity with standard software. (If you've been wondering why new hotels, motels and apartment blocks all over the continent look like Disney hamburger booths, wonder no further.)

3. **The exhibit designers:** The exhibit modules that housed the various pavilions were meant to be neutral housings for the fair's "real" content – the exhibits. That's the official explanation, and one that arrived late in the design process, to cover senior management's growing disinclination to fund architectural innovation. Expo spokespersons insisted, when it became clear nothing else was happening, that the fair's true content was going to be in the exhibits.

This was true in one sense, but misleading in several others. Generally speaking, the exhibits were more disappointing than the built forms. In almost all cases their content was predictably secondary to the media used to present them, and most were crashing bores.

4. **The administration:** This group ultimately exercised the most

powerful design influence, even though it is the most difficult to assign a clear identity. It consisted of Jim Pattison, the fair's board chairman, president and resident pixie, the right-wing economic and political interests residing in the Expo board of directors, the budget controllers, Jesus Christ Your Personal Saviour and Business Advisor, and Walt Disney. The various identities within this group are more or less interchangeable, since they're all fundamentally from the Disney mold.

EXPO'S WILD DESIGN ELEMENTS

Expo's design process did contain two peculiar elements that deserve to be noted. Neither received the attention they deserve, and they aren't likely to get it in the future, mainly because the B.C. government is trying to forget that Expo ever happened.

First, a normal procedure would have seen a design panel select project proposals from a list of candidates. Such a procedure would have ensured an overall coherence of design, and quite possibly a unanimity of materials and content. The Expo corporation simply didn't have time for design selection panels and the result was that there was no politically and conceptually consistent design strategy. Or, perhaps, it didn't have time *because* there never was any coherent strategy. What happened, therefore, was this: In most cases, blocks of the site were parceled out to various architectural firms, who then worked with the Expo design teams, the corporate clients involved, or with the governments that funded pavilions. The results were mixed, and the process was frequently more interesting than the product.

There's evidence that Expo's administration knew it had an architectural non-event on their hands early on. A year before the exposition opened, the Expo board decided that it did not want to fund an internal documentation of its design process. As a consequence, there is no consistent or complete source of documentary data available. How do I know that piece of non-history? In 1985, a week before he was fired as Design Chief, Richard Blagborne hired me to act as Expo 86's official architectural historian. I was told that my services were not required about 30 minutes after Blagborne was fired.

The succeeding waves of Expo's in-house design teams produced at least one recurrent design element that sets Expo 86 apart from its two immediate predecessors, the 1984 fair at New Orleans and Japan's Tscuba fair in 1985.

The New Orleans fair offered up just one coherent aesthetic element, the Wonderwall. The Wonderwall was a seamless Disneyfied web of simplified cartoon images meant to cover up infrastructure and to provide food and other consumer opportunities. The Wonderwall got a lot of positive attention, probably because nothing else at New Orleans was even remotely worthy of it. Most of the attention came from architects, who were intrigued by the technical virtuosity the Wonderwall displayed in covering up the weaknesses of an awkward site. The theme plazas at Expo 86 pretty much imitated the design parameters of the Wonderwall, with predictable results. They were spectacular, visually stimulating (from a distance), and without content.

Tscuba was typified by its exhibit modules. Properly looked at (with one eye on the structure and the other on the images revealed by the structure) the modules were black boxes. In fact, they were conventional Butler buildings with shiny, closed outer surfaces. Inside, the modules were entertaining but ultimately closed technologies – a perfect image of the way Japanese corporations tend to present themselves and their products to the public.

The architectural imagery presented by Expo 86 was quite different from both of these, and considerably less seamless. One reason for this was the absence of a coherent body to govern the fair's presentational aesthetic. The other reason is more interesting. Anyone looking out across the Expo site could have noted a startling dominance of external structure – pipes, gantries, etc. The site embellishment done by John Perkins recognized this, and instead of trying to hide infrastructure behind slick facades, it extended the effect in a series of thematic tower gates throughout the site. This dominance of external structure lent a curious tentativeness to the site that sharply contradicted the official message. My own speculation is that it was an unconscious registering of the reality most British Columbians face, whether in the overloaded professions or in the dying resource-extraction industries that fuel the B.C. economy. This part of Expo's imagination accurately registered both the uncertainty and the distrust of the smooth entrepreneurial elan projected by the rest of the fair. Or maybe it was just cheaper to do it that way.

THE FIRST REAL ENCOUNTER WITH WALT DISNEY

A return to Bruno Freschi and the early period of Expo's design leaves us gazing warily at the most spectacular remnant of the fair, the Expo Centre. Together with the fountain in Stanley Park's Lost Lagoon to the west, Freschi's Golfball forms a polarity, or dumbbell, in the downtown core. Never mind that the connecting road on the east side of this piece of urban abstraction, the Georgia Viaduct, curves to the northeast, away from the Golfball, thus making the dumbbell recognizable only at night from an airplane, and then only by closing one eye.

The Expo Centre is one of Expo's three permanent structures, and it was designed to become, in Freschi's phrase, an urban legacy. Inside it are a number of high-tech theatres, including an Omnimax, and another, smaller theatre where, during Expo, people voiced their opinions electronically on what they liked and didn't like about the presentations they saw. It's a spectacular building, but originally it was meant to be quite a lot more spectacular.

Early in the design process, Bruno Freschi commissioned an outrageously expensive and perfectly silly short film aimed at selling his concept of the design and purpose of the Expo Centre. A few months before Expo opened, I saw this film, and heard an embittered but carefully politic Freschi outline what he'd had in mind. He'd designed the Expo Centre to have an external television screen, and to have it connected to something he called a "teleport", which was, when you cut the techno-rhetoric from what he was saying, a huge satellite receiving dish planted in the middle of False Creek. The teleport involves the sort of technology you can now get into a suitcase at a cost of about $10,000, but never mind that. It would have been a great monument, and Freschi was very much interested in making monuments. This would have been Vancouver's own Statue of Liberty. Never mind that it would receive only incoming messages, and would say nothing at all about liberty except that in the Global Village, no one has any. "Never mind" was the unacknowledged secret motto of Expo 86.

The demonstration film featured a lot of vividly coloured computer-generated graphics, but seemed to have little to say except that the geodesic dome model was a symbol of "universality". As a demonstration of what universality might be, the film treated us to several more minutes of puerile graphic progressions that probably resemble what Disney World would appear like to someone on LSD. After watching the film, I couldn't help feeling that it was a good thing Freschi had been stopped when he was. His teleport was not built, and neither was the external television screen.

The last time I was in Hazelton, B.C., which is among the most beautiful landscapes in North America, I counted 27 teleports atop houses on the Indian reserve there. As a result, the place was virtually deserted. The residents were inside their houses, living halfway between Atlanta and Michael Jackson. As for the external screen on the outside of the Expo Centre, the legacy it would have provided raises the rather macabre image of the citizens of Vancouver wandering down to the Expo Centre on Friday night to watch prime-time American programming from Los Angeles on the big screen, perhaps going inside first to register their electronic opinions as to which program they want to watch next week. Some legacy. Some monument.

Freschi's plans were cut back because they were too expensive, not because the Expo Board disagreed with them in any substantive way. The Expo Centre, both as originally conceived and as eventually built, resembles no other building on the planet so much as the geodesic dome at Disney's EPCOT Centre at Florida's Disney World. What Freschi meant by universality, unconsciously or not, *was* Disney World. And more than anything else, Disney is what fueled the imagination of Expo 86, from Jim Pattison down to the most obscure budget gremlins.

A CONSPIRACY THEORY

Start by asking yourself what the content of Expo 86 was supposed to be. The official answer is that Expo 86 was a celebration of Transportation and Communications. Okay. Ask yourself why these need celebration, or how you would celebrate them beyond phoning your mother or flying to London on the Concorde. Then ask yourself just what was it *about* transportation and communications that the fair actually did celebrate.

If you take Expo 86 on its own terms, the answer you'll come up with before too long is – you guessed it – "Never mind." And why are you being so critical, anyway? There's no place for critical consciousness in a postmodern "exposition". And no place for it in reality according to Disney.

The Disney imagination has increasingly dominated the post-war expositions. And as its influence has grown, the expository content of the expositions has become either descriptive – as in "Wow, here's a spectacular machine!" – or purely formal – an exposition as a celebration of exposition. In other words, the subject matter of all communications is communications. Sure, new products and new technologies are tolerated and encouraged, but only if these produce bulk, colour and glitter. New or critical concepts are not tolerated at all. At Disney, the medium is the message, and the experience of the medium is everything. Those who object are party-poops. They may even be dangerous subversives. Never mind them.

Describing Expo 86 as Disney-dominated is quite a lot more than a metaphor. Almost the entire senior administrative staff was hired from Disney or from Disney-inspired projects. Many of the administrators were originally trained by Disney, and came to Expo from the corporation or from the moving apparatus that the recent succession of world expositions has created. As Expo took shape, these people became increasingly powerful. They took control because they were experienced managers of public imagination, and expert financial managers who knew precisely how much buzz could be bought for the available bucks.

Being afraid of Mickey Mouse and his pals may sound silly. Aren't there better, more easily assignable targets for our paranoia?

Don't kid yourself. With the possible exception of Ronald McDonald and the hamburger SS of the fast foods industry, the Disney corporation is the most pervasive cultural force in this civilization. Look a little more deeply into the Disney imagination, as reflected by the two major Disney installations in California and in Florida. Both depict a simplified world: a seamless web of beneficient organization and control where almost everything is good and right and harmless, and where the few wrongs that do exist are, if not righted, at least revealed in their most positive aspect. Everyone smiles, everyone is happy. The Disneyfied imagination does not admit human environments like those in Cambodia, East Timor or Lebanon, and there are no train wrecks in Northern Alberta, no tire fires in southwestern Ontario, no missile silos buried beneath Iowa's cornfields. Such environments and events are disappeared by Disney.

There is no pollution, no death or disease, no mental illness or stress permitted by Disney, and absolutely no tooth decay. Nobody is allowed to live out of shopping carts or in tin shacks or cardboard hovels. Such conditions reflect failure, and failure is not permitted. In Disney, technology is proposed as the solution to every human problem, and it is the antidote to every human frailty. Life is perfect within Disney's fantastical material milieu, and the individual is moved from positive novelty to positive novelty, each of which is sweet, smooth and entertaining. "Problems?" whispers the subliminal Disney mantra. "We don't have any problems. There are no unsolvable problems here."

Like I said, no critical content can be broached within Disney's reconstruction of reality. To criticize is to be negative. Thus, thematic content supplants critical consciousness. The themes are always celebratory, easy to consume and digest. Disney is the cultural adjunct to a strain of capitalism that has become the dominant economic force in the world we live in. Call it binary capitalism – Planet of the Franchises.

Disney seeks to create products and concepts which have a generalized and simplified appeal that can be duplicated easily and franchised out on a global scale. As such, Disney has become the alternative to the discourse communities and social contracts which are the bases of most Western democratic institutions. Franchise capitalism, with its capital and profit growth formulae, provides a means of avoiding the problem of having to make economic decisions people can live with by shifting all the decision-making out of the local arena. Disneyfication creates the virtual environments that nurture the McDonald's corporation, or the Amway religion, or any of a hundred other leading organizations that make up the post-ideological right. Franchisation provides the entrepreneurial frisson.

The Disney imagination operates in some very seductive ways. First, its attractively sterile images degrade the value of what is local and particular. Anyone can visit Disney, but only the chosen can live there. Both its model communities and the consumer deluge of Disney experience and consumer icons make less fortunate people unhappy with the hard-edged disorder of their ordinary environments. On a much more pragmatic economic level, franchises allow five to ten percent of the productivity and profits derived from local economies to be drawn off to head office, thus depriving them of the internal development and risk capital that enable internal growth in a local economy.

Hence, when we talk about the Disneyfication of Expo 86, we are talking, in a more or less direct sense, of the transformation of Vancouver into yet another teleport of the Global Village – an economic suburb of Disney dependent on external capital for economic growth and maintenance.

SOME SLIGHT AND INEFFECTIVE RESISTANCE

Disneyfication drew opposition from several groups during the Expo 86 design period. Because it downgraded – relentlessly and invariably – the value of local talent and industry, it was fought, for a while, by a not-very-successful alliance of artists, artisans, and their administrative advocates. In the end, enough of these people were co-opted by short term contracts to effectively silence them. Late in the process, the Expo planners even gave the artisans their own crafts pavilion, although probably only because some major corporate exhibitor or nation dropped out.

Surprisingly, Disney was resisted from within the Expo design apparatus by a few of the innovative people who wanted to present unorthodox but educative technological exhibits. One of the best ideas was to move a car crusher on site and use the crushed vehicles to build an accumulative sculpture. That idea, and others like it, didn't get to first base. Disney characteristically refuses conceptual risks of any kind, and it used predictable economic and aesthetic rationales to reject innovations that carried critical perspectives.

The car crusher and sculpture proposal wasn't Disney-acceptable because it didn't present a one-sided and seamless view of technology. Like human life, it was conceptually and physically messy. The technical difficulties involved in presenting the hardly revolutionary idea that cars don't disappear into the ether after they wear out would have exposed the public not just to the noise and fanfare of a spectacle, but also to the double-edgedness of technological processes. All such proposals were therefore buried by the Disneyites.

The Disneyites were also fought by those elements within the operations and design teams that believed that there ought to be some serious content to the exhibits. Design head Richard Blagborne, who is an Egyptologist, managed – I suspect by sheer force of character – to have an exhibit of ancient Egyptian artifacts included. Unfortunately, no other exhibits containing historically educative content or artifacts were funded by the Expo corporation. It left that, officially, to the national and/or corporate exhibitors, with results that had everything to do with the tourist industry and nothing to do with history.

ARE WE SUPPOSED TO BE FRIGHTENED?

Let me answer that question with another: what lay hidden beneath Expo's Disney design bias?

The answer is that it was the same thing that can be found at the heart of all franchise capitalism: a dreadfully simplified and misleading view of what human life and nature are about. Expo 86, as a whole, was a seductive monument to geopolitical globalism, which is to say, it was aimed at propagandizing consumerist values and habits, and at denigrating any other form of consciousness.

Globalist propaganda rarely acknowledges the reality or even the existence of the Third World, except where the Third World provides sanitized tourist facilities. It does not acknowledge the connection between technology and military aggression, or the fact that the international community spends a trillion dollars a year purchasing military weapons. And it does everything it can to obscure the technological and political uncertainty that is becoming our primary global and local reality. With its relentless onslaught of sterilized novelty, Expo was meant to dazzle us with what the future will hold, and at the same time to calm us about it. And that's exactly the effect it had on the vast majority of those who came. They did not go away better informed or wiser. They went away befuddled but happy, which is to say, in the cherished headspace of Social Credit and Mickey Mouse.

The primary impact Expo 86 had on the cityscape of Vancouver was pretty much the one the Disneyites designed it to have. It deliberately (and successfully) undermined indigenous cultural and economic practices. Not surprisingly, a startling number of local cultural groups and businesses ceased to exist during the fair. Most of those that were unable to suck up to the globalists suffered.

On a slightly larger scale, it isn't an exaggeration to link the current entrepreneurial frenzy in British Columbia to Expo, and it is no accident that a series of right-wing political victories have followed in the aftermath. Nor is it a coincidence that the B.C. lumber industry has been the site of one the most serious attacks on trade unionism in the postwar era – an attack that has been repeated in other sectors.

WHAT WAS EXPO MEANT TO ACHIEVE, AND DID IT?

Let's go up the scale from the venally local to the globally abstract. First, the government wanted Expo to globalize and stimulate the economy on a short-term basis. Expo was meant to serve as a billion-dollar greeting card for incoming capital investment and other entrepreneurial activity. Okay so far, sort of. Greater Vancouver did get a rapid transit system out of it, even if it is an outrageously expensive one that leading international experts say is a joke and/or a financial nightmare. Second, the same government wanted Expo as a springboard to get itself re-elected. Not quite so okay, because it worked, saddling B.C. with the stupidest premier it has ever had, and its most corrupt government. Given recent B.C. political history, neither were minor achievements.

The development community – in particular the architects and the in-house design teams at Expo who designed the various components – wanted Expo to secure or enhance their professional reputations. Since Greater Vancouver is currently facing a development hiatus – it is overbuilt in nearly all sectors – they have sought to use Expo as a catapult out of Vancouver and into international markets. Nothing wrong there. For Greater Vancouver's corporate business sector, the fair was regarded as an opportunity for a new level of networking and for some short-term profit-taking. While Expo was going on, for instance, the forestry giants were busy creating the world's largest clearcut in the northern interior, a treeless desert so vast it is, along with China's Great Wall, the only evidence of human life on this planet easily visible from outer space. Finally, the Disneyites wanted Expo to bring Vancouver into the "universality" network – into the mainstream of the Global Village, and under the benevolent supervision of the Dictatorship of the Entrepreneurs – under the EPCOT dome, in other words.

I'm an optimist, so I won't say that the Disneyites succeeded completely in their mission. In most of the arenas the results have been mixed. The government got itself re-elected, although the B.C. economy is in such a shambles that they may soon wish (along with the electorate) that they hadn't. Despite the state of the economy, the political right in B.C. is more certain of itself, and more convinced than ever of the correctness of the entrepreneurial model for everything from economic development to interpersonal relationships. An awful lot of people are more secure than they were before that everything is A-okay in the world, or that its unpleasant aspects can and should be ignored or avoided.

Certainly Expo has changed the outlook of a lot of people in Greater Vancouver, particularly the young. Many of them will probably go, or force their parents to take them, to a Disney facility in the next few years to see the "real" thing. I've noticed that they – kids and adults alike – have taken to bitterly complaining about any social event that doesn't include a fireworks display.

WHAT DID EXPO HAVE TO SAY ABOUT THE FUTURE?

Expo 86 did not take a serious measure of the future. It had no practical opinion about it whatever, except maybe that it is someone else's problem. Whatever people have taken it to mean, Expo 86 was an attempt to secure the present, and to reassure everyone that everything is just fine right now, despite the wealth of conflicting evidence. It was not an artistic event, and it did not present a coherent set of ideas, artistic details, or architectural features – not, at least, one that can be used as a basis for public discussions about how to face the future.

Perhaps the best thing about Expo 86 is that it has been more or less completely dismantled. Except for a domed stadium (to be used for eight semi-professional football games and a few religious revival meetings each year), the Expo Centre, the complex around the B.C. Pavilion, and the rebuilt CPR roundhouse, everything on the site came down before July 1987. The facilities that remain will probably become tourist facilities or fall derelict. Certainly none of them are needed by the local community, and they aren't flexible enough in their design to be recycled. Across the site, cost recoveries have been far below predicted levels. The much-vaunted exhibit modules, which were supposed to be recycled for community use across the province, turned out to be prohibitively expensive to move, and with one or two exceptions were simply torn down, along with the monorail and the other site embellishments.

The northeast portion of the site is slated for redevelopment by the site's crackbrained landlord, the crown corporation of B.C. Place, into a combination of retail, office and residential uses over the next decade. It will no doubt try to achieve this by selling the land to some developer at half its value. But since the development and land costs will be very high, there is unlikely to be much of a market for it. Expo isn't very pretty or useful anymore, not for anything. The western end of the site has no development planned, and seems destined to be derelict for many years.

In the aftermath the city of Vancouver elected its first right-wing government in years. And to admit the truth, the Global Village teleport Bruno Freschi wanted built seems to be in place even though it is located in people's minds rather than out in the middle of False Creek. But it is already obsolete, and maybe it always was, just as the Disney mission is ultimately a non-functional one.

There was a design party in Vancouver, a very expensive one that brought the city into the distant suburbs of the Global Village. Its consequences are everywhere, and the citizens of Vancouver are going to be dealing with them in whatever future they are still capable of imagining. If they don't redesign the mistakes made at Expo, there will be very little left of the city to work with.

Border/Lines

THE SATURATION OF THE PROFESSIONAL CLASSES

Some time ago, on the pages of a now-dead Montreal architecture magazine called *Section A*, one of Vancouver's prestigious architectural academics published a rebuttal of an article I'd written for the same magazine. My article had been a review of an exhibit of work by five well-known west coast architects. The rebuttal-writer so happened to be the curator of that exhibit, and he was ostensibly defending his honour and that of his exhibitors.

In my article, I'd criticized the architects for a postmodernist slickery that struck me as little more than pasted-on bric-a-brac with occasional references to the ideas that are currently fashionable among their corporate clients and the upper-middle-class political decision-makers who use architectural design to promote misleading images about what goes on inside modern buildings.

I'd made no particular attempt in my article to be fairminded, partly because it isn't my nature to be fairminded, and partly because the exhibit (and the curatorial hand behind it, which seemed unwill-

ing to go beyond "ain't all this creativity just incredibly neat") genu-
inely irritated me with its self-congratulatory smugness. The exhibit
seemed little more than a series of commercials pretending to be art,
and I didn't bother to pretend, as most reviewers do, that I wasn't hip
to the career goals and assists being picked up by the exhibitors.

Since I'm not a professional architect, I had nothing to gain or lose
from the attack. I think the editor of *Section A*, Odile Hanault, recognized my neutrality, and published the piece for precisely that reason. She knew that I wasn't exactly a newcomer to architecture, and
that I'd spent a decade working as an urban planner. I'd logged
enough time working with various urban professionals, including
architects, to have become familiar with the twists and turns of a
half-dozen urban professional vocabularies. In picking up that familiarity I'd sat through enough handshake meetings, stare-down
matches, self-congratulation sessions and other kinds of mind fuck-
ing to last me a lifetime. I'm painfully aware of how far from theory
street-level urban professional practice has drifted, and how much of
the "urban design" process goes on in the dark and dirty. In my article I simply admitted to the existence of that side of the professional
process, and it didn't seem to me that I was saying anything revolutionary. I just wasn't being polite.

The extraordinary venom of the offended curator's rebuttal very
much surprised me, because I didn't suspect that anyone in the professions actually *believed* in the bullshit they slung. His main tactic
was to attempt to discredit my professional expertise, and thereby, I
suppose, to discredit my article. Architecture, to paraphrase what he
said, is an extremely complex and sensitive professional field, one
that responds to and is shaped by the complexities of urban life.
Since it is so important and so complex, he continued, it can only be
understood by professional experts, which is to say, those who are,
er, intimate with the profession. The profession should therefore be
discussed, judged and regulated only by its expert practitioners, just
as it has been for most of this century. Amateurs are dangerous, he
implied.

Then he went on to describe why, as amateurs go, I was a particularly dangerous one. I won't repeat the really yummy details, except to note that at one point he made the Nixonesque gesture of implying that I was a commie radical. As his crowning put-down, he implied that I was nothing but a sleazy pimp for my own chocolate phrases. Most of the things he thought were grave and killing insults are things that, as a writer, I'm proud of. But that is beside the point. So violent a response indicated to me that I hit an exposed nerve, and a *privileged* exposed nerve is always worth scraping on. Besides, I'd just heard an apparently well-educated and sane man suggest that the firebugs should be in charge of the firehall.

Subsequent to the publication of his rebuttal, I've discovered a disturbing inability among my acquaintances in architecture to respond to the general issue of the meaning, rights and duties of professionals. The issue is worth repeating in its barest formulation: *Is architecture (or any other profession) a subject matter best kept within the purview of professionals in the field?*

Astonishingly enough, those who will answer the question with a resounding yes are ascendant across our civilization, and have been for most of this century. Professionalism, and the attitudes and public values associated with it, are treated with exaggerated respect, so much so that most of us don't question the profound ways in which professionals affect us. We live with the results of that unquestioning respect every day, and, I fear, we may soon have to live with it in considerably more unpleasant ways. For one thing, professional sanctity has begun to generate an extremely dangerous corollary attitude: professional services are to be provided in such a way as to service the professional community.

The most transparent instance of the effect of this corollary in Canada is the way the medical profession has used its privileged position to centralize medical facilities in close proximity to the personal residences of the doctors and, I suppose, to the offices of their stockbrokers and real estate agents. To rationalize this highly undemocratic arrangement, they have formulated a cost/efficiency argument that no government seems able to penetrate. It has made medicine, along with the banks, one of our few active growth industries. Along the way, they have also been ensuring that medical facilities are *not* being provided in the areas where they are needed, which is to say, where their patients actually live.

In Greater Vancouver, for instance, a new megafacility for the treatment of children's ailments was recently built on the west side of Vancouver, despite that wealthy area's small and declining child population, and the fact that the suburbs now hold the majority of the city's population along with a considerably greater and growing percentage of the region's children.

The official reason given for choosing the west-side site was that it is close to existing medical amenities. But the real reason, one suspects, is that the doctors didn't see why they should have to drive their Mercedes and Porsches all that distance to collect their $100,000-plus a year.

Similarly, a recent court decision has headed off an attempt by the government to channel incoming doctors to the areas that need them. Ignoring the rights of those who consume medical services, the courts ruled that this is an abrogation of the doctors' entrepreneurial rights.

Entrepreneurs the doctors have become. In 1983, after a restraint-minded government negotiated their fee structure downward, the doctors responded by billing more frequently. The result was a de facto increase in average gross income of more than 20 percent. Nor is this an isolated case. Other professions, with varying degrees of success and efficiency depending on the degree of service monopoly they have, enjoy the same self-regulating isolation from the economic, political and social realities that face the rest of us. And that is just the tip of the iceberg.

In other countries, self-regulated professionals operate with similar privileges. During the 1970s, the Argentine military became the envy of military professionals across the world, spawning a whole new set of professional and ethical procedures that are currently being followed wherever bananas will grow – practices that are, I suspect, dreamed of in many countries where bananas are still kept in the fruitstands and supermarkets. Infra-agency incarceration of political enemies, the administrative technique of "disappearing" dissenters, and the creative use of helicopters in the interrogation and disposal of suspects were all pioneered by these self-regulating Argentine professionals. Thirty thousand people died in the process, although the exact number, ironically enough in our world of statistical exactitude, will never be known.

Admittedly, my example of what can happen when overzealous and unrestrained professionals are let loose on a civil population is an extreme one, but as an illustration of what an overabundance of entrepreneurialized professionals can create, it has more validity than most of us realize. What occurred in Argentina took place at least in part because the upper echelons of the military were overcrowded with trained, ambitious professionals able to operate more or less outside public control and the rule of law. Luckily, we do not have Argentina's history of political violence, but what we do have is an overabundance of professionals in nearly every field except the military. Our professionals are, for the most part, operating under the same marginal levels of public supervision and they are, to all appearances, struck with a similar if less violent entrepreneurial spirit.

Because an overabundance in the professional classes is unprecedented in modern civilization, and because it is a phenomena grounded in sociology rather than ideology, it has been hard to read. For the most part, the northern industrial democracies operate as they have for the last century: educated professionals are universally regarded as a crucial ingredient of social and economic well-being, and are accorded automatic privileges and an aura of social dignity, even though for a decade now graduates in most fields have had to scramble for employment – often unsuccessfully – like common wage labourers.

Among architects, competition is perhaps the most fierce, and the unemployment levels are highest. Only the truly gifted or well-connected graduates now find work as architects. The rest end up as draftspersons or builders, if they choose to stay in the general vicinity of their training. Many of them abandon the profession altogether, and become entrepreneurs of one sort or another. Depending on who one talks to, architecture is currently facing either a kind of Armageddon in which only the genius and warrior classes will prosper, or it faces a ten-year hiatus in which only prudent and well-managed firms will survive. Certainly our commercial and residential infrastructures are now overbuilt, and are running on the system's inability to brake itself. We can't go on much longer building public facilities we can't support economically, and sooner or later the pension funds – which continue to fuel the housing industry almost by themselves – will be forced to ingest the feedback coming from the real estate market and will change their investment policy. Architecture is unlikely to maintain anything like present employment levels.

Educational professionals are in perhaps an even uglier predicament. At the universities, which grew massively during the 1960s and early 1970s and then abruptly ceased to grow except in instructor/student ratios, the faculties are larded with mediocre and overpaid academics shadowing their considerable wage and workload privileges. They're protected by self-serving arguments about academic freedom and a tenure system that has lost most of its integrity and credibility. Few universities have hired new junior faculty in a decade, and most are tottering with intellectual senility.

The college and trade school system, which took in and employed the later products of the same professional growth splurge that earlier filled out the ranks of university faculties, have become proletarianized. These institutions are loaded with burned-out teachers fighting among themselves for students on the one hand and job security on the other. Like the universities, they are responding to saturation and reduced budgets by protecting their upper echelons, and are even more subject to the same simultaneous decay and loss of credibility with the public.

In the elementary and secondary school system, the problems are different, but the situation is no less dismal. In the face of threatened budgets and fewer students, there has been an an accelerated exodus of teachers from the classroom that has resulted in the creation of an artificial middle-management bureaucracy that is as savage as it is intellectually sterile. Governments and parents alike seem bewildered by the covert battle that is taking place between classroom teachers and the middle-management entrepreneurs in this ersatz meritocracy.

Education budgets don't appear to be shrinking because the political consequences of cutting them are still unacceptable to governments, but classroom sizes are growing, high-contact professional and sub-professional services are being replaced by video-based rote teaching technology while the middle managers argue with disgruntled three-R conservatives within government and among the public over whether our children should be educated to live in Disney World or in the 19th century.

It is more difficult to gauge the impact of saturation among legal professionals. For one thing, the entrepreneurial spirit has been around in this profession long enough for Shakespeare to have made one of his characters suggest killing all lawyers as a way of lessening corruption, and most of us have heard the old stories about disaster-chasing lawyers or the more recent gags that tell us that sharks don't bite lawyers as a professional courtesy. A more serious indicator of the effects of saturation might be the massive increase in civil litigation in the last two decades and the increasing tendency of government, business and labour to seek the solutions to political and moral problems through the courts.

The internal workings of the legal profession are the most vigorously protected from public scrutiny, and this is not likely to be

altered as long as the profession continues to generate as large a percentage of our elected representatives as it does now. For a time, a
decade ago, the profession seemed bent on providing universal and
relatively democratic access to legal justice, and to its credit, it has
landed on the liberal side of most issues involving the provision (or
withholding) of rights and privileges in society. But since about
1980, legal aid budgets and legal education programs have shrunk
considerably, and the profession has been ineffective in fighting the
cutbacks. A cynical view would have them preoccupied with their
investment losses, or transfixed by the promise of entrepreneurial
opportunities afforded by the ongoing constitutional crisis and the
legal bureaucracy it seems to be engendering, and by the Americanization of Canada that seems to be the program content of the current
federal government.

Social workers – a loose and proletarianized term for a wide variety
of professionals whose function is to prevent or redress the social
damage inflicted by modern technological society on the economically or culturally underprivileged – have long been a hotbed of professional entrepreneurs. The entrepreneurial opportunities in recent
years have withered on the liberal side of the field but have picked up
enormously on the reactionary side. As social subsidy programs
aimed at increasing the dignity and autonomy of the traditionally underprivileged sectors of society – the poor, the handicapped and the
elderly – are slashed, ersatz professions like criminology have
sprung up to provide different kinds of professional opportunities.
Criminology is typical of the new social work – a lard-filled and relatively client contact-free field whose purpose is to rationalize the
constantly shifting fashions in warehousing the growing sector of our
population that runs afoul of the law.

   The Rousseauian intellectual structure that originally generated
social work as a profession in the early part of the century has disintegrated into a self-serving entrepreneurial melee similar to the one
going on in education. The difference here is that, with its original

goal of effecting universal social justice lost or subverted, with its patchwork mandate reaching into almost every other service monopoly, and with pressures created by the decrease in general wealth, bureaucratic body-snatching and careerism are openly accepted and even subtly encouraged.

One signal of this is the outbreak of utterly bizarre cases in which social protection agencies have violated the rights of individuals, some of them no doubt with justification, but others bearing remarkably transparent evidence that the agency involved was creating business for itself. What society is being subjected to, as these professionals run around drumming up business for themselves, is a phenomena that could be called "pathology fads", aimed at detecting heretofore hidden social abuses. Recent revelations about undetected child molesting, anorexia nervosa and incest may turn out to be as much the result of this kind of hysteria-creating professional entrepreneurialism as depictions of real societal problems. The methods used to identify and seek out perpetrators and victims are reminiscent of the Spanish Inquisition, and the presence of professionals who apparently have nothing better to do than to dream up more complicated labels for their clientele makes the comparison to past authoritarian religious tyrannies still more credible. Treatment programs for the victims and villains alike, I note, fall far short of the diagnostic industry, and that is a good indicator that something fishy is going on.

Money is the primary fetish of our society, and, not surprisingly, the financial sector has pulsed out a whole hierarchy of professional specialists for itself – almost in direct proportion to the growing recognition that no one really understands how money works. While there is appropriateness to this response, it also contains some brutal ironies. The proliferation of economic think-tanks is an illustration of how an economic system, faced with the collapse of its theoretical base and with growing public distrust of its working, sets up self-serving agencies to generate predictive opinion about what it would *like* to see happen. The purpose and methods of these agencies have become increasingly politicized and less grounded in research and theory as their predictive accuracies descend to the level of sheer absurdity.

Similarly, the field has generated an army of professional experts in tax evasion and manipulation. This is occurring at the same time as governments almost universally operate the tax system as if it were a Micronesian cargo cult, trying to attract industry with tax concessions, each of which are instantly cancelled out by parallel concessions from competing governments elsewhere – all without ever questioning whether governments *should* be competing with one another to attract a tax base. If one accepts that increased government borrowing is a de facto form of taxation, the insanity of this approach is immediately evident.

I could go on, but by now any reader can easily follow the effects of saturation and entrepreneurialization into any profession and collect his or her own data. The inevitable conclusion is that the professions are out of control. The question to be asked from here is not whether it is a problem, but what can be done about it?

Without a fundamental re-examination of the role of the professions – one that focuses on the responsibilities of the professions to the public rather than on the rights of individual professionals and how much screwing around they can do under the cover of professional privilege – not much can be done.

First of all, in most instances, the professions are linked to service monopolies. These service monopolies are, to greater or lesser degrees, regarded as basic social rights by most of us, which means that we have forgotten that our ability to fund them is directly related to the productivity and wealth of the body politic. In the long run, none of them can be demand driven. As that wealth and our productivity levels have stabilized in the last decade or so (in some cases the wealth has begun to shrink) the levels of service – at least theoretically – ought to have stabilized or begun to shrink.

There's very little evidence to suggest that much rational response to this built-in limit is going on from the inside. Service monopolies, if the self-regulation of their professional practitioners was operating rationally and in the interest of society, should be responding to this new situation on a disinterested ethical basis. But this isn't happening. The sole response so far has been some adjustments in service delivery, and even that, so far, has mostly just set the dogs to fighting among themselves over scraps.

This is happening, in part, because literally all the professions are saturated. There are already too many hungry professionals around for us to expect them to acknowledge that there are limits to their numbers, and that these limits are dictated by economic factors beyond their range of activity.

Second, a lifetime of privilege has made most professionals far more interested in protecting their upper-middle-class splendour than in serving the public interest. Almost every profession has reacted to saturation within its ranks by ignoring or setting aside ethical responsibilities, and by engaging in entrepreneurial activities within and outside its area of social control and influence in order to enlarge its individual and collective portion of the pie.

Third, and harder to grasp, is that with the saturation of the professions there has occurred a corresponding decay in theoretical research and the ethical thinking that, when professionals were rare, was nearly as useful to the enhancement of democracy as their professional functions. If this extremely dangerous decay is to be reversed, it can be accomplished only if the general public demands a coherent accounting of professional procedures and privileges.

It is unlikely that the professions can effectively regulate themselves any longer. Aside from the outbreak of entrepreneurism, their only response to saturation thus far has been to specialize. Specialization is an accurate reaction to complexity, but in an environment that is highly competitive and self-regulating at the same time, it rarely accomplishes what it sets out to do. It simply generates more work. Specialization too often has become a means of generating business, despite the isolated and always very well-publicized miracles it produces. Miracles make good news, but they rarely address essential problems. And with the fashionable but simple-minded political enthusiasm for solving all our difficulties by "unleashing the entrepreneurial spirit," it is becoming socially and economically dangerous to address essential problems. Someone might lose their BMW.

Perhaps we have to reintroduce the notion of "public service" and "general good", however awkward and difficult and unfashionable those concepts have been made to seem. They should be made the subject of an ongoing and broadly based *public* debate, one that the professions themselves should have initiated long ago but didn't. Such a debate may not sound like fun, but it offers more possibilities than what we are currently doing, which amounts to little more than fighting over a rapidly emptying gravyboat, and selling our children into bankruptcy and the slavery that will result from it.

Because this is still a democratic society, the obvious place to start the debate is at the cornerstone of democracy: public education. During the 1960s, the entrepreneurial spirit in education began to generate an entire and isolated field of education – now called, variously, "adult education" or "continuing studies". Despite the altruistic intentions for this kind of education, it is dangerously misdirected. A quick glance through the courses offered by any of the many existing programs will show that the vast majority of courses offered are aimed at self-improvement, with either a vocational or recreational focus. People can learn to be more vocationally skilled or competitive, or more self-satisfied, ruthless, and physically fit. The subject matter offered is usually asocial and at times, frankly antisocial. This attitude toward adult education is now invading the more traditional forms of education as well, but it is right here at the level of voluntary education that it ought to be challenged. Instead of promoting individual skills, the curriculum should be discussing the fundamental values of our society and the duties, as well as the rights, of citizenship. And that is the proper subject matter of the liberal arts, a.k.a. the humanities.

We all know that the liberal arts are out of favour right now with governments and the corporate sector, who seem more transfixed than anyone with the idea that only the entrepreneurial energies of society will renew our overextended economy. Most politicians and corporate captains are convinced that it was the liberalism of the fifties, sixties and seventies that got us into this mess in the first place. They're wrong. It was the educational cowardice of the liberal arts in failing to uphold this crucial ongoing debate that helped get us to where we are. Governments may be right about the value of entrepreneurs, but only in a much more limited sense than the one being applied. The biggest culprit in creating the present fix has been the entrepreneurial activity within our saturated professional classes, along with the governments who extended service monopolies to unregulated professionals without regard for the fact that the ability to provide services has a very direct relation to general wealth.

Only a renewal of liberal arts curricula can generate the general debate over professionalism that is needed to bring the professions back to the realities the rest of us have to account for. But first we have to deprofessionalize the liberal arts, which have richly earned a large measure of their current low status within the mire of petty departmental turd-polishing at our universities and schools.

Liberating them will take an enormous effort and a great deal of political courage. But they are the appropriate subject matter for adult education, and adult education, in the deepest sense, is what we must have.

Border/Lines

POSTPROFESSIONALISM IN ART AND ARCHITECTURE

The first thing the dictionary has to say about the word "professional" is that it is that which pertains to, or marks entrance into, a religious order. One might be tempted to laugh at this definition, or shrug it off as an obsolete etymology. I don't because I've learned that words have a way of meaning what they say, and of holding onto their etymological roots in curious ways. An infidel examining architecture and art from outside the comfort of their respective cloisters can easily see the extent to which both disciplines have been closed in the 20th century by something called "professionalism".

If one ignores, as infidels do, the body of theoretical justification for practice, one can see two main things at work in contemporary architecture: A) something called functionalism turning space into commodity and utility, and ultimately into an accounting procedure, and B) at a slightly different level of action, individual architects attempting to create personal and career signatures across our cityscapes with their built forms.

In art, which has a far less immediate and physical proximity to the economic mainstream, one sees professionalism characterized by a brutalizing search for novelty and a burgeoning body of theory that is largely uninterested in testing itself against parallel theory in any other discipline.

Not to be a party-poop, since both disciplines obviously provide a great deal of delight to their practitioners, but the muteness of architects and artists on the subject of multidisciplinary issues is a big problem. No matter how much fun everyone is having, neither architecture nor art can really be considered effective intellectual forces within contemporary civilization. Architecture, for the most part, slavishly reflects conventional political and economic values. Art, which historically has been a powerfully affective political and cultural force, has done its best in recent decades to divorce itself from the entire question of public value. Tradition, historical mandate and product in both direct them toward taking a leadership role in the public arena. Only the privileges they've recently gained as professionals encourage them to ignore those inherent responsibilities.

To some, it may seem extreme to blame professionalism – until we remember that it is in the nature of a privileged class to resist change and to be willing to consider literally every alternative before examining the content and public effects of its practices and rituals. And while art and architecture have been around for a while, professionalism, at least as we have come to experience it, is a relative newcomer. In architecture and the arts it emerged largely as a protective reaction to the increased complexity of copyright and to the onset of litigative activities over intellectual property. In the past few years professional organizations have become – sometimes unwittingly and reluctantly – the Waffen SS for the commoditization of creative intelligence.

Happily, there are exceptions. Joost Bakker's work in Vancouver over the last decade has amounted to a direct confrontation with this new strain of professionalism, in both his activities as an architect and as a visual artist. As an architect he's a former colleague of controversial Toronto contextualist George Baird, and the author of most of the best design elements of Vancouver's Granville Island development through his association with Norman Hotson. As an artist, he owes very little to anyone except perhaps Saul Steinberg's sense of irony.

People on the West Coast, accustomed to public architecture dominated by Arthur Erickson's monuments to cocaine and other ego-expanding substances, immediately found the federal government-funded Granville Island easy to understand and use. Operating on the contextualist principle that the object of an architectural exercise is to integrate newly built form (and the changes that go with it) with the most humane elements of the existing environment, the design of Granville Island recycled the vast majority of the existing buildings, retaining in particular the original (and relatively inexpensive) metal cladding. The project is unified aesthetically by a system of brightly painted steel pipe lintels and cedar poles, which aren't, as with most postmodernist design, simply there for decoration. The pipes are utility conduits, and contain much of the island's electrical infrastructure. They also serve a startling variety of other pragmatic uses.

Bakker also carefully tried to retain whatever industrial activities remained economically viable on the island – to the point where Emily Carr College of Art and Design is situated in rebuilt industrial buildings next to a large sand, gravel and concrete operation that has been a fixture on the island for decades. Hence, the small island retained a multiplicity of activities that specifically excluded, at least until the tourist bureau discovered that it was a potential attraction, only tourist facilities. The art students still cheerfully dodge cement trucks on their way to classes, and the shoppers at Granville Market now have to bear the ordure of being photographed by Japanese tourists while they shop for local vegetables and salmon steaks, but the original ideas behind Bakker's design still make sense.

The most important of these ideas is that Granville Island ought to be designed for use by the local community, not to please the tourism industry. The successful realization of this idea is evidenced by the fact that Vancouverites took to the place with an enthusiasm that is well beyond the wildest dreams of the funding agency. It is also no accident that tourists like to visit the place. Granville Island is among the few places in Vancouver where outsiders can discover how people on the west coast of North America live, work and play. It is arguably the one spot in the city where Vancouver acts like other great tourist cities – Florence and Paris come to mind – because once there Vancouverites confidently go about their local business and politely ignore the presence of visitors.

Bakker's work as an artist has matured with his work on Granville Island, becoming a kind of critical analog to what he discovered while working on the design. In July 1982 a small gallery in Vancouver's Chinatown, the Fitch Gallery, featured a dual exhibition of his work. Included were cibachrome details from Granville Island, architectural drawings from a number of other sites, a series of sixteen 8½ by 11 drawings, four of which had been silkscreened in a larger format, and three recent drawings.

The conceptual centrepiece of the exhibition was the series of sixteen drawings. The set constitutes a remarkable serial meditation upon contemporary public imagery. By focusing on graphically simple images, like those of telephones, the nose-cone and undercarriage of the Concorde, and other commercial yet heavily symbolic graphics, Bakker built a disturbing narrative that grows in intensity as he puts together different combinations, adds and deletes images. He holds the series together visually through the use of three primary industrial colours – red, blue and yellow.

His narrative is disturbing not for its novelty or its creativity, but because it forces us to see everyday images we ingest subliminally in a new and ironic light. We see the utility of familiar objects, but we also see their alienating and often threatening character. What was most interesting about them was that the drawings are virtually the opposite of artworks that employ recombinant signature imagery (for example, dairy or leopardskin "themes") by which so many contemporary visual artists have sought to "privatize the market" on their chosen images. In looking at Bakker's drawings, one is brought, not to an appreciation of the artist's flamboyant creativity, but to the fact of one's own manipulation by commercial and corporate graphics. The impact of the drawings is as much a critical one as it is sensory. Bakker is interested in what he is seeing around him in much the same way, one suspects, as those first visual artists scratching on the walls of the caves at Lascaux and Altamira 20,000 years ago. He wants to know what is essential in the things around him, and what isn't. And he is about equally motivated, as I suspect were those early cave artists, by uneasiness as by creative delight.

Most people involved with art (or architecture) tend to treat everyday graphic images and symbols as a vulgarity to be ignored. Most of the few who actually work with them embroider on them, tacitly humanizing and softening their manipulative characteristics – their simplicity and their impenetrability – and tend to lose sight of the idea that their truth is ironic and not rhetorical. Bakker's drawings deal directly with those characteristics, simultaneously exaggerating and simplifying their graphic properties by confining them within industrial colours that are less subtle than the ones these images would have in their "natural" socio-economic environments. Then he removes their opaqueness by using them in disjunctive and often ominous combinations, showing us their true content, and the ways in which they hide their real message and function.

To say that Bakker's architectural work operates the same way is only a slight exaggeration. What he has sought to do is to remove from his designs any obscurantist symbols and signatures. His pipe system is considerably more than design flash meant to signal "Hey! This is me!" What it signals instead is that there is a functional unity within the project that invites users to manipulate the system for their own practical purposes. Other aspects of the design are less spectacular, but all share the same respect for integrative public utility and cost effectiveness. One wishes that the designers who plotted out

Disney North across the waters of False Creek had demonstrated a similar degree of critical intelligence.

In the catalogue for the Fitch Gallery exhibition, Bakker quotes a recent interview in *New Age* magazine with Fritjof Capra:

> Today we live in a globally interconnected world in which biological, psychological, social, and environmental phenomena are all interdependent. To describe this world appropriately we need a new paradigm – a new vision of reality – a fundamental change in our thoughts, perceptions, and values.

Such a fundamental change requires, among other things, a postprofessional stance on the part of architects and artists. Joost Bakker's work in both fields is a move in that more public-minded direction.

Section A

ARTHUR ERICKSON'S UNIVERSE

There is a story about Arthur Erickson that oldtimers at Simon Fraser University like to tell. In the late 1960s, the story goes, the sculptor Henry Moore was brought to Vancouver for the dedication of one of his pieces. He was taken to see the then-new campus, and during the visit he was asked by one of his house-proud hosts if he'd ever seen anything quite like it. Moore seemed startled by the question, and mulled over his answer carefully. Finally, he said that it had the aspect of a stage set, and that its grandeur rather reminded him of the Nazi podium at Nuremburg Stadium.

Moore was no doubt expected to describe Simon Fraser as "startlingly original" or some other slogan of *haute commercial* architectural gibberish. When he said pretty much the opposite, and, worse still, seemed to be implying that it was inspired by the Nazis, there was a shocked silence among the assembled dignitaries. So Moore elaborated, explaining that the Nuremburg podium was based on the tomb of one of the Egyptian pharaohs, and that Erickson's design was, well, deeply interesting because it contained such a range of echoes.

Simon Fraser University was Erickson's first really major project, and the one that launched his career into an international orbit. It's also a project with which I happen, as an SFU graduate, to have a long and intimate acquaintance. It was an intimacy that began in an odd – and very ungrand – way.

All through the winter of 1966, the university's first, I watched too-thin sheets of glass from the main concourse's huge canopy buckle and then crash down into the concourse. Some junior engineer had made the silly but potentially lethal error of basing the canopy's weight-load factor on the average annual snowfall for Vancouver International Airport, forgetting that Simon Fraser is perched atop Burnaby Mountain, where Vancouver's famous winter rains frequently turn to snow.

Within a few years there were considerably more profound and well-publicized problems at Simon Fraser. They didn't have anything to do with engineering blunders, but a lot of us who were there at the time recognized that they were indirectly Arthur Erickson's doing. Sure, the student and faculty radicalism that erupted at Simon Fraser in 1968 was part and parcel of the times. But it happened at Simon Fraser with such elan because Erickson's design for the campus ensured that every student and faculty member had to pass through the same central courtyard on the east side of the main concourse to get to any location on campus. Erickson deliberately designed Simon Fraser to create an integrated community of teachers and students. And that's exactly what his design produced.

Despite its historical echoes and its minor engineering glitches, Simon Fraser was a remarkably skilful piece of utopian traffic design. The problem with it was that everybody – from the government to the faculty through to the students – quickly discovered that B.C. wasn't quite ready for a democratic utopia. As a matter of record, since 1969, every single addition to the university has been aimed at decentralizing the traffic patterns Erickson designed into it.

The university's administration quickly acquired a secure building away from the main concourse, a series of cafeterias was built in other areas of the campus, and eventually even a faculty club was built far from the old hub. Twenty years later, SFU has three times the number of students, but Erickson's central courtyard is nearly always deserted.

Those Simon Fraser anecdotes are perhaps apocryphal and slightly contradictory, but then just about every story you hear about Arthur Erickson is. The Henry Moore story seems to tag Erickson as a crypto-fascist, the courtyard story as a utopian democrat, while the falling glass canopy anecdote indicates that he suffers from a certain careless inattention to detail. Yet if I'd begun by examining his residential designs the first thing I would have cited is his often exquisite attention to fine detail.

Only one view of Erickson is consistent: as Canada's foremost exporter of design architecture, and arguably our most creative architect, he has made architecture a topic with more substance than the technical shoptalk and careerism that occupies most professions – and most other architects. Whatever you may think of Erickson or his buildings, you'll have to admit that he's our only architect to have consistently engaged public – and intelligent – controversy with his designs. Vancouver's Simon Fraser, the Museum of Anthropology on Point Grey, the Robson Square/Vancouver Art Gallery/Courthouse complex, Toronto's Roy Thomson Hall and Yorkdale subway station, Ottawa's Bank of Canada building, the Canadian embassy chancery in Washington, D.C. and the Canada exposition pavilions at the 1965 Tokyo Trade Fair, Expo 67, and Osaka 70 have each and all been focuses of sometimes furious debate.

An astonishing number of people across the Canadian professions have Erickson stories to tell, along with heady opinions about him and his work. Fellow architects tell the best stories, but invariably they tag their critical remarks with a "don't quote me" admonition. Their discretion isn't merely fear, envy or architecture's version of the "professional courtesy" made infamous by lawyers. Even the most unfriendly remarks about Arthur Erickson are grounded in respect for the man and his buildings, and a recognition that no single anecdote can capture his whole story.

In Vancouver, it isn't just professionals who get involved. Nearly everyone has a definite opinion about how good or bad Erickson's buildings are. As often as not, the building under discussion isn't even Erickson's. The assumption is that if a building is unusual or interesting, it must be one of his.

Vancouver's Douglas and McIntyre recently published a large and rather splendid volume of Erickson's work, with a text written by the maestro himself. The book offers a wide (and indexed) selection of Erickson projects, built or proposed, from the residential designs with which he began his career in Vancouver in the 1950s to the grandiose projects in Saudi Arabia and elsewhere that died at the proposal stage or are yet to be built.

By itself, Erickson's text makes the book worth the price of admission. He's framed it as a kind of architectural autobiography, one that he takes pains to point out is framed in mid-career, even though he's now in his mid-60s.

Certainly the timing is appropriate. Erickson's 1986 Gold Medal from the American Institute of Architects deservedly puts him where he's always wanted to be – in the upper echelons of international architectural design. Yet there's another, darker side to it. The award came just as Erickson's international operations have run into severe financial – and some say creative – difficulties.

For the past several years, while the Miami Vice school of bric-a-brac architecture has been slithering down to its lowest postmodern common denominators, Erickson's operations have had to undergo a "rationalization" process that has apparently come close to sinking him. The publication of this book, in a sense, is the official announcement of a new phase in Erickson's career – one that presumably sports a new, leaner operation to match the practices and priorities of our meaner, leaner times.

The book's foreword, by critic Peter Blake, has the pleasant virtue of being remarkably free of the usual structuralist newspeak that makes so much architectural criticism unreadable. I'm grateful for that, and for the minor mercy that neither the Queen Mother of West Coast art and architecture, Doris Shadbolt, or her literary equivalent, George Woodcock, were brought in to explain what a charming guy he is at their cocktail parties.

Instead, Blake contributes several useful items to our understanding of Erickson. First, he points out that Erickson is almost unique as a third-generation modernist who remains faithful to the functionalist canon of the movement while consistently attacking its limitations.

In case the term "modernism" isn't very informative to you, let me give a simplified definition and brief history. Architectural modernism, when all the lard is cut from it, is the humanistic belief that form should follow function. That still might sound like technogibberish, but it really isn't. It means that a building should be as visually and dynamically efficient as possible – functionalism, it's called. A modernist office building, for example, should have no waste space, no irrelevant ornamentation, and no frivolity of any kind – because that's how modern business is, har, har. Business and building alike are there to make profits for their owners and shareholders, and they should look like it. Testosterone under aesthetic control, in other words.

In its brightest light, architectural modernism is a signal of grave but basically democratic intentions. But since it's also a style, it often drifts beyond its functionalist roots, or, more often, fails to express them accurately. Most of us have worked in or at least been inside modernist office buildings long enough to discover that the inclusive – and sealed – environments they create aren't very efficient or humane. The best modernist residential design, on the other hand, has been much more successful than its predecessors in addressing the functional issues of light orientation and access, demographic reality and local materials. In both design areas, commercial pressures have tended to make a mockery of both the style and its intended goals.

The theorist of the first generation of modernists was Le Corbusier – the Kahlil Gibran of architecture. He viewed the human body as a mystical mechanical model – a dictum that modernists have been stumbling over ever since, because capitalism and humanism simply don't mix except in theory. The significant activists of the first generation were people like American Louis Sullivan and other, usually more bloody-minded utilitarians of something called the Chicago School – the builders of the first sleek slab office buildings around the turn of the century. These inclusive rectangular cages of iron and steel, with their often-overpowering visual signatures, have become synonymous with the best and worst elements of our economic system – at once extraordinarily dynamic and idiotically singleminded.

The bright lights of the second generation were Frank Lloyd Wright and the Bauhaus group in Germany. In different ways, both injected a strain of social democratic sobriety into the older generation's enthusiasm for simple mechanized efficiency. Wright built a few remarkable residential buildings aimed at integrating human and natural environments, and tried – mostly unsuccessfully – to introduce a rather more complex concept of what functionalism should entail. The Bauhaus architects built more buildings than Wright, and extended their range of design to furniture. Bauhaus buildings and furniture share the same abstractly functional qualities. Their modestly scaled and understated buildings all look like pharmaceutical factories and the furniture looks terrific but isn't, finally, very comfortable.

Elements of both the first and second generation of modernism melded in the post-war boom. The rapidity of development and pressures of profit-taking created the absolutely vulgar functionalism of most of our urban architecture – the familiar deserts of three-storey walkup and highrise apartments, and the petrified forests of monolithic office buildings vying to impose their corporate signatures upon one another and upon the cities they look down on.

Second to Erickson's modernism, and perhaps still more usefully, Peter Blake identifies him as, at heart, a landscape architect. He notes Erickson's debt to Frank Lloyd Wright, who first introduced the notion of integrated communities of earth, light, and human beings to soften the brassy elan of Le Corbusier's enthusiasm for mechanical efficiency.

Erickson's text repeatedly speaks about the need for architecture to integrate natural environment and community, although his understanding of both terms often seems remote from the actualities of day-to-day life. His most ambitious and innovative projects – the University of Lethbridge, Vancouver's Museum of Anthropology and the Robson Square/Courthouse complex, Ottawa's Bank of Canada building, and even the Canadian chancery in Washington – have each been grandly abstract integrations of either historical or natural imagery with contemporary functional necessities. They're most successful, unfortunately, at a distance and in the abstract.

Vancouverites are grateful to Erickson for the Robson Square/Courthouse complex because it saved them from a planned fifty-storey monolith. And to be sure, Robson Square is a modernist integration of environment and community at its best, particularly the outdoor landscaping – which is Erickson at his best. In the heart of a city, it creates a variety of multiple-use spaces without disturbing the purely functional patterns of the area. In theory, anyway.

It is the adjoining courthouse complex that betrays the limitations of his modernist impulse to integrate theme and function. The vast glass canopy and cascading greenery frame a light-filled gallery that is symbolic of the majesty of our justice system – comforting to the judges and intimidating to the criminals. Like Robson Square, it is also a spectacular piece of urban landscaping, at least from the Hornby street perspective – or, better still, if you're flying by in an airplane. But by burying its workers in almost wholly subterranean and encapsulated work environments, the complex betrays the simple-minded Le Corbusian vision of social hierarchy that has caused many of us to question the basic values of modernism: how and when is efficiency truly efficient, and for whom?

From the beginning, Erickson has used his gift for spectacular landscaping to impose a conspicuously personal signature on his built forms. In that respect, he's a typical modernist. Yet the aloof abstractness in almost all of his larger projects is a truer element of that signature, as if he were trying to root modernism in a deeper reality than mere commercial efficiency. Cynics may opine that he reads too many Italian design magazines, that his conceptual landscapes are too dependent on very large budgets or that his variety of egotism is one we can no longer afford. There is an element of truth in all their criticisms, but still, they're selling him short. The signatures his buildings impose are qualitatively different from the purely commercial signatures imposed by modernist environmental aggressions such as the Toronto Dominion's "Dark Towers" in Vancouver and Toronto. However ostentatious Erickson gets, he's never designed a building with a revolving restaurant on its roof and you can be damned sure he never will. For all his egotism, he seems utterly impervious to vulgarity.

Still, the aloof abstractness of his landscapings contains a weakness. One gets the sense that he'd cheerfully rip out a real forest in order to represent the *idea* of one. The part of him that is pure modernist rationalist too often gets it on merely with the part of him that is a pure Jungian astronaut in search of archetypal reality. Too often he forgets that the ground of the sacred is neither egotistical signatures nor authoritarian grandeur but the day-to-day necessities of work, food, and shelter.

Aside from its exhibit spaces and theatres, Robson Square is chiefly a place where office workers go to sit in the sunlight – a commodity Vancouver isn't exactly overwhelmed with. For all its panache, the facilities there don't address the actualities of day-to-day urban life nearly as fully – and flexibly – as say, Hotson/Bakker's less flamboyant but equally ambitious Granville Island, which integrated a wide variety of semi-derelict industrial activities and buildings with incoming consumer and cultural outlets – at a fraction of the capital cost. There, the viable industrial activities remain on the renovated site, the private sector reaps the desired profits, and the people and the government love it.

Erickson's past achievements – and mistakes – leave me wondering what the next phase of his career will produce. The last few years have seen more and more grandiose proposals, and rather fewer completed structures. Will his streamlined operation and the economic realities of the 1990s produce a scaled-down – and more sensitized – regeneration of his modernism? Can there be another Arthur Erickson – even if it is Erickson himself?

If it were up to me, I'd say yes on both counts. And to explain why, how about another Erickson story?

In 1960, Erickson bought a modest bungalow in Vancouver's Dunbar area, apparently much to the delight of his new neighbours, who anticipated a stunningly redesigned paradigm of modernism – one that would raise property values throughout the neighbourhood.

When Erickson duly had the existing house bulldozed, the level of anticipation rose even higher. Then he lined the excavation hole with plastic, filled it with water, built a solid seven-foot cedar fence around the lot, landscaped the pool and environs with characteristic elegance – and moved into the small garage he'd been quietly renovating at the back of the lot since the beginning of construction. A quarter century later it remains among the city's most exquisite dwellings – all on a fifty-foot lot.

That side of Erickson doesn't excuse the errors, the excesses, or the jet-setting egotisms. But with postmodernism's pastel-tinted hot milk beginning to curdle in our veins, a rebirth of modernist values – with a redefined sense of how complicated human sensibilities and needs really are – is probably the only alternative. Arthur Erickson has the vision, the daring and the sensitivities to play a leading role in that rebirth.

Saturday Night

INTERESTING
TIMES

It is already a truism to characterize the 1980s as the decade when almost everything around us got bigger, faster, and more electronic – and life got emptier. As a society, we're at the faded and jaded end of economic and sexual revolutions that promised to make life sweeter and freer and somehow only made it meaner. Meanwhile we're trying to liberate ourselves from racism, misogyny, and from a whole series of largely self-inflicted psychosocial and economic ailments caused by trying to have our cake and eat it too. Most of what we gained in the 1980s, it often seems, is the obligatory liberty to consume the "revolutionary" commodities of our choice. Perhaps we're being punished for our gluttony in just exactly the way Dante would have predicted – by being forced to go on eating far beyond the point of nausea. In the middle of our liberated consumer frenzy, perhaps as a misguided reaction to it, we've seen an increase in left-wing right-minded people telling us just exactly what we ought to consume, and which genuflective postures we ought to assume while we're stuffing our faces and impoverishing the planet. These are, as the double-edged Chinese expression has it, interesting times.

Neither individual artists nor the arts were excluded from the "interesting" developments of the 1980s. The arts have become a veritable flood of expressive (albeit politically correct) liberties, and in every discipline the boundaries of expression are drifting further and further from everyday realities and closer to either pure commercialism or pure self-absorption.

It seems to me now that much of it is misdirected and mistaken. Liberating ourselves – as citizens or as expressive beings – wasn't the crucial issue that faced Western society in the 1980s, and it will be less so in the 1990s. There are now at least two issues with global implications on our collective plates that demand intelligent response more urgently than do the vicissitudes of liberty. One of them is how we will cope with steadily diminishing material resources, and why, in what is supposed to be the Era of Total Information, we are being deceived all the time. It is those two issues, and what we didn't do about them, that will make the 1990s even more "interesting" than the 1980s were.

On the whole, artists don't seem to have noticed that they didn't do their job in the 1980s. Yeah, sure, we all know that artists are supposed to be in dreamland, right? Well, yes and no. Yes, artists are supposed to ignore the day-to-day racket of society's machinery. But the reason they're supposed to ignore it is because their job is to ask those barely tangible but thoroughly crucial questions that everyday life moves too fast to allow most people time to consider. Over the last decade, unfortunately, most of the artists I know were engaged, formally and otherwise, in addressing the issues of twenty or thirty years ago.

What I'm suggesting is that the 1980s happened to artists pretty much as they happened to everyone else. Artists got caught up in the gears, the antennae went down, and as a result, the impacts of the decade's changes, technological or otherwise, remain largely unexamined. Word processors, to talk about something I know about, became generally available for writers during the last ten years, offering enormous gains in efficiency, and perhaps more important, enhancing writers' abilities to think and research laterally. Yet the overwhelming majority of writers continued to work in unchanged genres and formats. Technological advances in other disciplines seem to have met with a similar response – slightly greater volumes of the same old shit, or if you prefer a politer phrasing, in an era of diminishing budgets, more efficiently produced obsolete products.

Let me put this inattention in its least attractive light. For several decades now, artists in Canada and across Western Civilization have acted like frogs in a pond, each trying to scramble onto the centre of the lily pad in their chosen genre or discipline. They've been so busy at it that they haven't noticed that the pond is being landfilled for a global shopping mall.

A more kindly explanation is that the changes are so enormous and the forces behind them so powerful that no response was possible. Well, that would certainly let the artists off the hook. But as Primo Levi once said, the genius of human intelligence is to have the daring to *attempt* to foresee everything, and if the arts are not to completely lose their place as the vanguard of that genius to the amorality of tactical and applied science, kindly explanations will not excuse the lack of foresight. A brief look at four interesting arenas of change in the 1980s might provide some insight into what happened, and what might be in order in the 1990s.

HERITAGE ARTS

The 1980s saw the emergence of what, for lack of a better term, I'll call *heritage arts*. In Canada, this development is partly an ironic consequence of the generosity and conservatism of our cultural funding agencies, partly a side-effect of the curatorial and critical senility that has been growing in our universities since the mid-1970s, and partly a consequence of communications technologies that have evolved far more rapidly than our conceptual tracking and application of them.

As we head into the 1990s, Canada can boast an artistic output that outstrips the wildest dreams of those enlightened souls who recognized, back in the 1950s, that if Canada didn't learn to protect and nurture its indigenous arts and culture, we'd soon be Americans, or worse. Today, Canadian artists, in literature, music, theatre and painting, are probably as good as any in the English-speaking world. So far, so good. The problem is that most of them operate within genres and formalisms that have changed very little since the beginning of the century and which are now in an advanced state of either petrification or putrefaction. At worst, most of what our cherished artists do has become a heritage activity not significantly different from those museum exhibits where tourists can go to watch antiquarian artisans making butter or milking cows the way it was done a century ago.

I can't think of any artists who aren't guilty to a greater or lesser degree, so there's no purpose in pointing the finger at anyone in particular. It's enough, to get very blunt about the discipline I know the most about, to say that Canada may have more skilled 19th century poets and novelists per capita than any country in the world. We have too many poets who write obscurely of their private feelings about nature or their sexuality or their ancestors, and we have too many novelists who compose intricately symbolic 300-page tomes about the same essentially trivial things. Even though it makes me uncomfortable to think about it, I can't help wondering what our poets and novelists would be doing had they been encouraged – or forced – to face the technological and economic music the way less privileged sectors of society have had to. It's interesting that our governments, a significant part of our banking sector, and our artists are the only ones privileged – or in the case of artists, marginalized – enough to still be in dreamland.

TELEVISION

Everybody in Canada – artists, educators and elected representatives – misjudged the essential nature and mission of television, including, I think, Marshall McLuhan. A cold-eyed scan of television viewer demographics testifies to the medium's actual mission: to reduce us to a Disneyfied lowest common social denominator, to sell us standardized merchandise and ideas, and to ship the profits to New York and Los Angeles.

The neurological effect of scanning a pixel matrix alone makes the expression "educational television" as much an oxymoron as "military intelligence" has proved itself. For most human brains, twenty minutes of television produces an overabundance of alpha waves, rendering the owner/occupant incapable of critical response.

The television industry has recently responded by inventing its own unique genre: infotainment. *Entertainment Tonight* is probably the purest expression of this television newthink. It treats presidential elections, natural disasters and celebrity galas alike, judging them strictly in terms of how many glitzy images they produce, and whether the images can be franchised off into profitable peripherals.

Infotainment ought to be a natural medium for artists, since that's really what art is supposed to do in the first place – delight and teach. But left to its own devices and constrained by solely its commercial mission, infotainment will tend to go on atomizing the information it communicates and alienating the audience it informs. During the 1980s, more and more people have come to rely on infotainment's homogenized, third-rate factualities as the building blocks of public and private reality. Scary business.

It isn't a coincidence that Canada is woefully weak in television and in the other electronically and economically charged artistic media. With the exception of documentary film-making, Canadian artists produce an unacceptably minute share of what Canadian audiences see and hear – only fifteen percent of our music, and two to five percent of our theatre films and prime-time dramatic television programming. The good films we do produce are rarely distributed beyond specialized and largely non-commercial markets. The television drama we do produce, usually folksy stuff like CBC's *Beachcombers*, either make us look more rustic than we really are, or they do their level best, like CTV's *Night Heat*, to make Canadian cities look and act like downtown Cleveland. Where Canadian artists are getting into the mainstream at all, they're doing it by edifying and pleasing Jack Valenti and the Disney corporation, not the Canadian public.

SENILITY IN THE UNIVERSITIES

Twenty-five years ago the humanities departments of the universities were both a breeding ground and a training school for intellectuals and artists. Most of the faculty were then young and energetic, and more than a few of them were practising artists themselves. They constituted a quite viable avant garde, creating an atmosphere of intellectual and artistic ferment for the young. Since then, the good artists have left in disgust, and those who remain have gotten old, tenured, and more interested in pensions and mortgages than in ideas. So too, the old ferment has mostly been drunk off or has turned to vinegar, and there has been virtually no renewal beyond a renovation of administrative and curriculum Stalinism aimed at tossing the entire Euroclassical canon in the nearest dumpster and replacing it with New Age good intentions and territory-crazed minorities demanding to be given the full rights of citizenship without having to learn what the duties are. Meanwhile, Marshall McLuhan's dream of an electronically enhanced convergence of intellectual and artistic disciplines has evaporated in budget wars and academic tenure committee hearings.

Since about 1975 all but the most docile elements of the succeeding generation have found themselves shut out of any ongoing connection with the universities. Young artists and intellectuals have been forced to sell their skills in the marketplace, an experience which is sometimes edifying but more often simply humiliating, or they've ended up in proletarianized junior college and trade school teaching jobs, with workloads too heavy to allow them to practice or to keep up with the advances in their disciplines. Some have been able to live along the economic and social margin with the aid of grants, short-term commercial projects and teaching, but that's all.

At the beginning of the 1980s the economic panic created a corresponding panic in higher education that cut heavily into humanities budgets, and effectively closed the doors to all but the most conservative programming. Humanities faculty shadowed their jobs and the universities began to act like tweedy trade schools – hardly an atmosphere conducive to free and experimental thinking.

Without complaining about the justice of any of this, the consequences have been deadly for both the humanities and for the arts. Intellectual ferment simply doesn't take place in a system where administrative "accountability" sweeps are everyday terrors, and curriculum planning is part opinion polling and part pep-rally for the Chamber of Commerce. The ongoing trade-school mania is producing technically adept formalists with an intellectual repertoire that is dangerously out-of-date. Graduates tend to have one eye on the marketplace and the other eye on the centre of the ragged lilypad their embattled but exhausted teachers are losing their hold on. Few are equipped – or disposed – to look at those big questions that are their correct milieu.

ECONOMIC 'REALITIES'

Back at the beginning of the 1980s, I had the opportunity to hear a hotshot developer pitch a major new development to the urban planning agency I was then working for. The developer explained the mix of residential, office and retail space he had in mind, and what it would do for the local and regional economy. Quite naturally I asked him what kind of community he envisaged, and what kinds of cultural facilities he intended to integrate into his design. He replied, with a cold grin I still haven't forgotten, that the desired cultural activity in Canadian society during the 1980s and 1990s was going to be retail shopping, and that his company intended to put its cultural investments exactly where people wanted them. I was the only person in the room who winced.

That, in a nutshell, is the attitude with which the private sector has approached art and culture during the 1980s. And although government arts funding has been maintained, sort of, through the decade, the same attitudes have been creeping steadily into the public sector. This is particularly true at the local level, where the arts have become synonymous with the performing arts, and are treated as a somewhat unruly adjunct to the tourism industry.

The arts are indeed good for tourism, simply because they provide about the only colour we have that is more permanent than the colours of Benetton. They're also a more powerful contributor to local economies than most people recognize. But that's not all they are, and it's not why people, across history, have put up with the eccentric behaviour of artists, who can be a major pain in the ass, as artists know better than anyone. The arts – and artists – exist so that people can see, without the lies made necessary by short-term expedience, just exactly who they are, where they are and what they are up against. Everyone forgot about this in the 1980s, and we'll all have to pay the price in the coming decade if the arts don't start addressing those larger issues with a lot more rigour and daring.

Someday, the 1980s are going to be looked back on with horror as a kind of crackpot Dictatorship of the Entrepreneurs. The glorification of the marketplace reached a degree of fervour that borders on religion, and has created a free-for-all of opportunism throughout society that has landed us in a glitzy free-trading Global Village that hides its seamy side and its injustices and its cruelties – exactly the opposite of what art is supposed to show us about ourselves and our world. But at both the practising and administrative levels the arts have bought into it without enough second thoughts.

Ah, it's all so depressing. 1990 is here, and the countdown to the millennium is about to begin. The 1980s saw the disintegration of a coherent political vision of Canada and its arts and culture. The implicit challenge the decade raised to the arts was to choose between those parts of our heritage that remain active and valuable, and those we must consign, with regrets, to the museums or the junkheap. But the truth is that artists just crawled under their covers and made no choices at all. Another decade of protecting the past and resisting any and all change will land both the arts and the artists permanently in some dusty exhibit hall with the milk pails and the butter churns. Canada will have an artistic and cultural heritage, but our cultural and political future won't simply be cloudy and unexamined, like it is as we head into the 1990s. It won't exist at all. And that will be "interesting" beyond our worst nightmares.

Globe and Mail

INDEX

Printed in Canada